WAR AND SOCIETY IN THE SEVENTEENTH CENTURY

THE WILES LECTURES
GIVEN AT THE QUEEN'S UNIVERSITY
BELFAST 1956

WAR AND SOCIETY
IN THE
SEVENTEENTH CENTURY

BY

SIR GEORGE CLARK

SOMETIME PROVOST OF ORIEL COLLEGE, OXFORD

CAMBRIDGE

AT THE UNIVERSITY PRESS

1958

PUBLISHED BY

THE SYNDICS OF THE CAMBRIDGE UNIVERSITY PRESS

Bentley House, 200 Euston Road, London, N.W. 1

American Branch: 32 East 57th Street, New York 22, N.Y.

©

CAMBRIDGE UNIVERSITY PRESS

1958

Printed in Great Britain at the University Press, Cambridge
(Brooke Crutchley, University Printer)

CONTENTS

v

PREFACE

THE first four lectures in this volume are the Wiles Lectures delivered in the Queen's University of Belfast in October 1956. To the Trustees of this foundation I owe deep gratitude, not only for the opportunity of giving the lectures, but for much kindness and hospitality during my visit. That I found the occasion not only enjoyable but impressive was due to the founder of the Trust, Mrs Austin Boyd, to Sir Eric Ashby, Vice-Chancellor of the Queen's University, and to Professor Michael Roberts, its Professor of Modern History. The last lecture was honoured by the presence of the Governor of Northern Ireland, Lord Wakehurst.

In accordance with the terms of the Trust a number of scholars were invited to the lectures and took part in discussions which followed them. Besides the members of the University History Department and other members of the University staff, there were nine visitors, Professor T. W. Moody, of Trinity College, Dublin; Professor J. Lough of Durham; Professor F. J. Fisher, of the London School of Economics; Dr G. A. Hayes-McCoy, of the National Museum, Dublin; Mr S. H. F. Johnston, of University College, Aberystwyth; Dr F. L. Carsten, of Westfield College; Mr John Ehrman; Mr Peter Laslett, of Trinity College, Cambridge; and Mr H. F. Kearney, of University College, Dublin. The discussions were lively and general; I hope the participants will recognize from the printed text how much I learnt from them, and I must record my sincere thanks.

Preface

To these four lectures I have added two others which have been published previously. The first, on the Barbary Corsairs, illustrates part of the argument of the Wiles Lectures. In its original form it had serious faults, and these were pointed out to me by Sir Godfrey Fisher, whose book *Barbary Legend* is to be published this year. I have tried to express my thanks to him by undertaking the necessary revision. The other lecture, the Creighton Lecture delivered in the University of London in 1948, is of wider scope but on a related subject. It has been out of print for some time. For permission to reprint these two lectures, and to use some passages from an article, I have to thank the Syndics of the Cambridge University Press and the Editor of the *Cambridge Historical Journal*. Finally I owe many thanks to my wife, who has relieved me of the troublesome task of making the index.

G. N. C.

OXFORD
March 1957

CHAPTER I

WAR AS AN INSTITUTION

THE subject which I have chosen for these lectures has occupied my mind from time to time for many years past, and in various books and articles published at intervals since 1921 I have touched upon it.[1] The invitation to deliver the Wiles Lectures, for which I must express my deep gratitude to the Trustees, gives me an opportunity to review and correct my opinions and to submit them to the judgement of the distinguished company which is assembled here.

The period I have chosen is the seventeenth century, not, of course, the exact hundred years, but the period which historians commonly treat as a unity, including, at the beginning, the earlier stages of affairs which were then in progress and, at the end, the whole of the reign of Louis XIV of France, who died in 1715. I shall try to keep in mind the heritage which the seventeenth century carried along with it from the past; but, except for that, as far as possible I shall keep within the period. Some of the things that I shall say about the seventeenth century are also true of the twentieth; others are not. I shall not mention these identities and differences, and I even wish to exclude them from my argument. The present state of the literature of this subject seems to indicate that we shall positively gain by restricting our

---

[1] A list of these is given in the Appendix (p. 151 below). In the footnotes to the present work references to these books and articles are given without the titles but with their numbers in this list.

attention in this way. There are military and political histories in which wars are treated one at a time; but the historians who have tried to understand war as a social activity or an aspect of civilization have commonly set it in an evolutionary framework. Hegel, Comte, Herbert Spencer and Karl Marx have successively influenced these historians. It is easy, again, to find books which trace the mutual effects of war and capitalism over long periods. There are other books which trace the development of the rules of international law recognized at the time when they were written, and books which present international transactions as steps towards some future summit, perhaps the peaceful settlement of international disputes or perhaps the perfecting of total war. Any one of these interpretations of our period in the light of others before and after it may turn our attention away from some of the characteristics of war as it actually was, and it is the concrete character of the wars of Europe that I wish to examine. For this purpose even a century is a long period, but if we can see it in focus it should provide a firm beginning for comparisons with other periods. If I do not intend to make any such comparisons in these lectures except once or twice to make my meaning clearer, it is not that I underrate their value. Hypotheses about evolutionary or cyclical changes in the relation of society to its wars are fruitful elements in the thought of our time, and, especially during the last eleven years, since the explosion of the atomic bomb at Hiroshima, historians in many countries have studied the nature of war as a social activity with a new sense of urgency. I suspect that some of them have reached their conclusions too hastily, and that in this matter we still need modest inquiries limited in time and space.[1] I cannot, indeed, pretend to offer a finished study; in some parts I have attempted to survey or to revise the results of research, but in others I have reached only a programme for further investigation, and a number of disconnected queries. But I hope to establish three definite conclusions and possibly even a fourth.

Perhaps the most natural approach to such a subject is through the writings of the time itself, and in the seventeenth century much was written about wars and about war in all the literatures of Europe. We can hardly expect to learn much from the second-rate and the merely imitative writers; we must beware of the pitfalls of generalizing about a multitude of particulars, and we must not overestimate the adequacy of literature as a report on life; but, with these precautions, we may gather some useful preliminary notions from literature in general, including the uninspired routine writing of every day. There are many simple, and natural, emotional reactions to war, and we find two of them endlessly reiterated, as they are in the writings of so many ages. The first is the response to what is glorious in war, to the feats of courage and endurance and to victory. In Latin and in all the vernacular languages innumerable poets and prose-writers expressed these moods. Little of all this appeals to modern readers; it may be strong and sincere, but we are apt to find the idiom of that age formal and stiff and dull. Seventeenth-century writers were not occupied, for instance, with the individual man and woman as those of the Romantic period were, and so when these works have to do

---

[1] An example is D. Loenen, 'Polemos', in *Mededelingen der Koninklijke nederlandsche Akademie der Wetenschappen, Afd. Letterkunde*, Nieuwe Reeks, Dl. 16, no. 3 (1953), which deals with ancient Greece.

with persons it is not with Homeric heroes or Byronic heroes, but with prominent commanders. The odes and panegyrics and inscriptions may still be admired, but they no longer stir emotion. They are like the two great faded tapestries in the old House of Lords in Dublin, representing the relief of Londonderry and the battle of the Boyne. If we feel emotion when we contemplate them it is not they that move us but the knowledge and the memories that we bring to them. Nevertheless, we can be sure that they expressed real pride in real military virtues, just as we can be sure that the second spontaneous reaction to war, the reaction of pity and indignation, was equally authentic. The two were never far apart. Shakespeare expressed them both, and if his patriotic exultation is more commonly remembered, the other reaction fills more space in his works. In the official utterances of court poets and court preachers, in what may be called standard public literature, the proportion is reversed; but both ingredients are there. They are not toned down as they have been in some other periods. The writers did not shrink from the crudity of the contrast which they saw in war, as in all human life, between *grandeur* and *misère*.

It is, however, justifiable to ask whether literary men in the seventeenth century were not notably insensitive to the darker aspects of war. It seems, for instance, that in spite of their allegiance to the classical tradition they did not appreciate the treatment of this side of the human tragedy by the great classical authors. Among all the writings on the miseries of war, one stands alone in its relentless directness, the *Trojan Women* of Euripides. It was accessible by itself or in editions of the works of Euripides, in Greek and in Latin; but I

4

cannot find that anyone in the seventeenth century responded to its appeal. The dramatist Nicholas de Pradon published a play on the same theme.[1] It was acted before
Louis XIV himself, who honoured it with his particular
attention and his applause. Pradon altered the story by
making Astyanax and Polyxena take their own lives instead
of being killed by Ulysses and Pyrrhus; that was too grim
for 'notre théâtre', he wrote, 'Nos mœurs sont trop douces
et trop éloignées de ces mœurs sauvages et barbares'. He
allowed Ulysses, after remarking that Agamemnon desired
Cassandra for his bride, to continue

> Je suis Roy, je suis Maistre et vainqueur comme luy,
> Enfin je dois céder à l'amour qui m'entraine,
> Je sens que malgré moi j'adore Polixène.

Pradon was second-rate, and we shall not find vulgarity like
this if we turn to what the great Racine did with the same
materials. A few notes of his on the *Trojan Women* survive;
we do not know whether he made any others, but these few
do not help us to determine what he thought of the play.[2]
His *Andromaque* shows that he was interested in its dramatic
technique, and he takes situations from it in which his
characters are stationed as individuals with passions and
duties; but there is not a trace of social criticism or of
Euripidean pity.

Other instances could be adduced to show that seventeenth-century writers were not merely swept into eloquence

[1] The Bibliothèque Nationale has an edition of 1679; I have used that in
Pradon's *Théâtre* (1695). The passages quoted are in the Preface and Act I, sc. i.
[2] R. C. Knight, *Racine et la Grèce* (s.a., published in 1950). I have to thank
Professor Knight for a most interesting letter in which he relates this matter to
the quarrel of the ancients and moderns and to seventeenth-century views of
monarchy.

by the glitter of victory, but convinced that the rights of conquest were ethically unquestionable. Corneille wrote straightforwardly: 'Le peuple est trop heureux quand il meurt pour ses rois.'[1]

These passages and the many others like them do not, however, justify us in supposing that the seventeenth century was insensitive to the sufferings inflicted by war. Corneille's words tell us more about his attitude to monarchy than his attitude to conquest. Racine, to say nothing of Pradon, saw Euripides through the opaque lenses of modern criticism and Senecan stage-craft. Another instance may show that literary forms which are now outmoded dull our apprehension of the feelings that writers tried to express. It comes from the German poetry of the period of the Thirty Years War. This poetry, with its religious phraseology and its classical allusions to Mars and Ceres and their likes, seems flat and conventional to a modern reader; but to appreciate it as it appeared in the princely *Residenzen*, where it found favour, is to recognize that it is sincere and even poignant.[2]

What the drama and poetry do show is that in the seventeenth century war was taken for granted as a fixed necessity of human life. This acceptance was not confined to imaginative literature but was equally characteristic of systematic thought. It is, indeed, as easy to misinterpret the systematic thought as the imaginative literature. It would be an anachronism to read the seventeenth-century writers on war as if they provided answers to the questions which modern

[1] *Oedipe* (1659), II, 1.
[2] See Irmgard Weithase, *Die Darstellung von Krieg und Frieden in der deutschen Barockdichtung* (1953), especially pp. 8–9 and 15.

students of society ask. Here also there were traditional precedents to follow. There was the medieval and Biblical teaching that war was a divine punishment for the sins of peoples. There were classical texts which scholars carefully discussed, such as the passage in which Thucydides distinguishes the real motives of wars from the ostensible pretexts.[1] But, whatever we understand by the terms, we shall often find seventeenth-century discussions of them disappointing. The underlying problems of the nature of political power and authority were central to many current controversies; yet when some of the greatest thinkers dealt with the causes of particular wars they were helpless. Thomas Hobbes analysed the causes of the English Civil War like the great thinker he was; yet even he had curious lapses. Both before and after the Civil War there were many disputes between the English and the Dutch, and one of the subjects was a very disputable English claim to the sovereignty of the Narrow Seas. On 14 May 1652 there was a naval battle. Hobbes wrote in the form of dialogue:

B. The war certainly began at this time; but who began it?
A. The Dominion of the Sea belonging to the *English*, there can be no question but the *Dutch* began it.[2]

Hobbes was one of the seventeenth-century thinkers who came nearest to the conception of social science as a study in which the whole should be understood through the interdependence of all its parts. Many others grasped something of this idea, and it had a rudimentary expression in two metaphors, that which compared society with an organism,

[1] See Hugo Grotius, *De jure belli ac pacis* (1625), bk. II, xxii, especially in the Annotata to the chapter.
[2] *The History of the Civil Wars of England* (ed. of 1679), pp. 246–7.

as in the fable of the belly and the members, and that other, congenial to the scientific mind of the later seventeenth century, which compared it with a machine. But few writers followed these ideas consistently and many failed to observe any connexion between the other sociological problems which they discussed and the changes from peace to war and back again. There is an instance of this in the work of the English Board of Trade. The foundation of this board was closely connected with conflicts about shipping losses during the Nine Years War. Its commission was dated 6 July 1696—a year and two months before the peace of Ryswick. One of its first tasks was the preparation of a report on the general state of the trade and manufactures of the kingdom.[1] This includes both an estimate of the existing position and detailed proposals for improving it in every possible direction. It was signed on 23 December 1697, and one of the signatories was John Locke. We should expect such a report in our own day to examine the effect of the war on 'the economy', and to pay attention to the special needs of the transition to peace. Instead, in this report we find only two allusions to the war, neither of them implying anything that deserves to be called thought. Nor must we assume that the writers had deeper reflexions in their minds but chose not to refer to them in that context. No seventeenth-century writer had any such developed conception as we normally accept of the organic interconnexions of the different elements of an economy. The French economic writer, Boisguillebert, wrote in so many words that foreign war was no obstacle to the restoration of general happiness; and that 'la paix ou la guerre étrangère n'ont nulle relation

[1] *Commons' Journals*, XII, 71 and 432 ff.

avec ce qui se passe au dedans du royaume à l'égard des tributs'.[1]

In these examples we see economists writing as if the outbreak of a war was like the change in a university town from vacation to term, which alters the flow of goods and services, but does not change the economic structure and in due course will easily be reversed. They took the coming of war for granted; they did not examine it: but our social thought treats it as a subject for economic study. Such a study cannot be content to treat each separate war as a self-contained occurrence, and its beginning as an event in a succession of events. For many writers, identifying a cause meant no more than pointing out that if some act or belief or condition had not been present or had not turned out exactly as it was, then there would have been no war. But they knew that if there had not been war at the exact time and place when it did occur, and between exactly the same parties, there would still have been wars. Milton, without having to explain it, wrote in a mere parenthesis: 'for what can war but endless wars still breed.' Granted certain assumptions, each war might have been avoided; but, so far from indicating how and why wars did come about, this only obscures the overriding truth that there would have been wars in any case. To keep the occasions of particular wars in their proper proportion we must recognize that in the seventeenth century war was not a mere succession of occurrences but an institution, a regular and settled mode of action, for which

[1] Although thus incautiously worded, the passage in question is intended to convey, reasonably enough, that fiscal reform need not wait for the coming of peace: P. le Pesant de Boisguillebert, 'Supplément au détail de la France' (? 1707), in *Économistes financiers du XVIIIe siècle*, ed. E. Daire (1843), p. 263. See also Appendix, no. 11.

provision was made throughout the ordering of social life. It was an institution in the sense that it was defined and arranged for by various prevailing systems of law, and also in a wider sense: the structure of society implied that it would recur.

To say this is more than merely saying, what we should be justified in saying after any review of the frequency and severity of its wars, that European civilization in the seventeenth century was a military civilization. It was that, and it was known to be that. Hobbes, like many other seventeenth-century thinkers, held that any society must include elements such as the family, and any civilized society certain higher elements such as religion, commerce and law or justice; he also argued that the relations between separately organized societies, even if these were civilized, would be warlike. There were anti-Hobbists who rejected his determinist view of human nature, and in their views wars might be occasional or accidental; but it is true of the social theorists in all the main streams of seventeenth-century thought that, like the imaginative writers, they took the institution of war for granted. Their thinking about war, including their thinking about its causes, was for the most part carried on within the framework of the traditional distinction between just and unjust wars. Jurists and theologians applied their learning and their acuteness to the Biblical and classical and medieval texts through which this distinction could be traced. It was not a simple and single distinction. Sometimes a just war meant only a war which conformed in its causes and conduct to what the law required if the legal consequences of a state of war were to ensue. In that case the belligerents could lawfully exercise certain rights over the goods and persons of their enemies as far as these were in their power and were bound to concede due rights to neutrals. But writers who were not writing about law, theologians for instance, meant by just war warfare that was morally justifiable; and when historians asked 'Who began it?' they often understood the question to mean 'Who was to blame?' If there were just wars in this sense, then it was compatible with a just ordering of human affairs by divine Providence that such wars should go on. When Richard Bentley, the great classical scholar, turned his powerful mind to confuting Atheism, he considered how Providence had led man upwards to *humanitas*, or civility. He saw that the use of weapons had played a part in this process; he amended Hobbes's account of the state of nature thus: 'We must consider withall, that (in the notion of Atheism) those Savages were not then, what civilized Mankind is now; but *Mutum et turpe pecus*, without Language, without mutual Society, without Arms of Offence, without Houses or Fortification; an obvious and exposed Prey to the ravage of devouring Beasts, a most sorry and miserable Plantation towards the peopling of a World.' He thought that a power, unrecognized by the Atheists, had given them the means of making war, but not so as to stultify all human endeavour. As an example of clear thinking I commend what he says about aerial warfare: 'And if Mankind had had Wings (as perhaps some extravagant Atheist may think us deficient in that) all the World must have consented to clip them; or else Humane Race had been extinct before this time, nothing upon that supposition being safe from Murder and Rapine.'[1]

The routine wording of public documents and the standard arguments of political writers did, indeed, imply that

[1] *Boyle Lectures* (4th ed. 1693), pp. 78, 163, 175.

peace was normal and war was an aberration from it. There was a favourite quotation from Aristotle that war is waged in order to bring about a better state of peace.[1] Joseph Hall, bishop of Norwich, wrote in the year of the execution of Charles I, and followed St Augustine[2] as he wrote: 'War is no other than a necessary evil, necessary in relation to peace; only, as that without which so great a blessing cannot be had.'[3] At the end of every war the belligerents agreed on a treaty, which usually recited in the preamble the evils of war or of the effusion of Christian blood and always provided in its first clause not merely for peace but for a peace welcomed with strings of adjectives such as 'good', 'stable', 'durable' 'sincere' and 'inviolable', in different combinations, and not least frequent among them, 'perpetual'.[4] No doubt these adjectives expressed the moods and hopes of the signatories; but the actual clauses of the treaties seldom implied anything but a negative view of peace as the absence of war. Once in a while some provision was made for peaceful change in the future relations of the contracting parties. In 1619, in the accord between the English and Dutch East India Companies, a common defence council was set up in Indonesia, and it worked successfully for a number of years. In 1654 when the Dutch made peace at Westminster, all such claims for commercial and colonial damage and injuries since 1611 as they were unable to settle in conference between themselves were left to the decision of the Protestant Swiss cantons;

[1] *Pol.* IV, 14, 1333a 35; 1334a 2 ff.
[2] For Augustine, *Civitas Dei*, XIX, 12, see H. Fuchs, 'Augustin und der antike Friedensgedanke', in *Neue philologische Untersuchungen* (1926), III.
[3] *Resolutions and Decisions of Divers Practical Cases of Conscience* (1649), p. 190.
[4] This was not so foolish as it looks now: a perpetual peace meant a peace with no fixed time-limit such as was usual in a truce.

decisions were duly made and accepted. But these were claims relating to the past, and no provision was made for arbitration on claims which might arise in the future. Few men grasped the idea of Grotius that true peace was organized co-operation. The treaty conception of peace was negative, while war was essentially positive; and it was on the working of this institution, or on the threat of its coming into operation, that Europe depended in much of the public business that might involve major changes in the relations of its States.

It may seem perverse to maintain that seventeenth-century thinkers in general took for granted the continued existence of war, when the text-books summarize various schemes for universal peace. These schemes, indeed, had no influence, because they all postulated action by the States which these States, from their very nature, were incapable of taking; but, quite apart from their being impracticable, the writers of these schemes themselves supply a proof of our contention that war was taken for granted. First of all, the truly pacifist writers supply it, those who believed that it was wrong for the individual man to kill as a unit in an army. Most of the seventeenth-century pacifists were carrying on a tradition of Christian pacifism which had existed for centuries side by side with the official theology of the just war. It had its own continuity which can be traced through the obscure records of heresies, and even through some of the great folios which scholars used, like the works of Erasmus. In the seventeenth century it was found, not among the churches, but among the sects, which lived apart from the affairs and responsibilities of government. But it was by no means a narrow or single line of thought. It appealed not only to Biblical texts and ethical principles, but to common sense and to respect for the common man. The first systematic Quaker theologian, Robert Barclay, wrote not only against rendering evil for evil, but also against going 'a warring one against another, whom we never saw, nor with whom we never had any contests, nor anything to do; being moreover altogether ignorant of the cause of the war, but onely that the Magistrates of the Nations foment quarrels one against another, the causes whereof are for the most part unknown to the souldiers that fight, as wel as upon whose side the right or wrong is'.[1] The author of these words also addressed a letter to the plenipotentiaries at the peace congress at Nymegen in 1678,[2] as John Amos Comenius had addressed those at Breda eleven years before.[3] The pacifists did incidentally and in a subsidiary way regard their problem as a problem of international organization; but for them it was a minor point that the secondary and more immediate causes of war might be removed by 'carnal' prudence and policy. They held, with Barclay, that the ground of war was the want of true Christianity. Fundamentally it was from this point of view that they condemned 'all wars and strife and fightings with outward weapons, for any end or any purpose whatever'.[4] They did not busy themselves with

[1] R. Barclay, *Apology for the True Christian Divinity* —— *Preached by the People in Scorn called Quakers* (Latin ed. 1676; English ed. 1678), propositions XV, XVI.

[2] *Epistle of Love and Friendly Advice to the Ambassadors of the Several Princes of Europe* (1717). The pages all have the marginal date 1677, in the autumn of which year Barclay wrote the work after a visit to Holland and Germany in the spring. He also sent his *Apologia* to the plenipotentiaries and their principals.

[3] *The Angel of Peace*, tr. W. A. Morison (*s.a.*), with the Latin text of 1667.

[4] These words are taken from a declaration of 21 November 1660 signed by George Fox and eleven others and presented to King Charles II. Although there were some militant Quakers before 1660, I cannot accept the unqualified view of Mgr R. A. Knox in his *Enthusiasm* (1950), p. 148, that the Quaker pacifism of the Restoration period represents 'a change of front'. George Fox's

projects for the peaceful settlement of international disputes. William Penn was exceptional in this as in many other respects. On the social and political plane, the others took the negative view of peace: to them it meant keeping out of war. The typical pacifist was another Quaker, honest Edward Coxere, who reports a conversation 'leaning on the ship's side' with his shipmate Richard Knowlleman, 'who had been a gunner of a man of war and left his employ on the account of fighting, and was counted a Quaker, yet (it seemed) would fight in a merchantman'. 'I asked him...if we should have occasion to fight, what must be done. His answer was that we might fire at the mast.... I knew that when we came board and board we had the men to deal with and not the mast. This would not serve.'[1]

There were, indeed, projects for perpetual peace, and in our own time they have become famous, although none of them had any effect when it was written. Most of these projects, however, are not schemes for universal peace. In one perfectly definite respect, they, too, take for granted the continuance and even the extension of the practice of war.[2] The imaginary Grand Design of Sully may be regarded as a reply to some of his French contemporaries who were writing that a State which does not expand must perish. Taken by itself, however, it was a scarcely disguised proposal for uniting the States of Europe under the hegemony of France, and their compensation for surrendering their

letter of 1654 to Oliver Cromwell states his pacifism clearly, with the positve reason for it, and he refused to serve as an officer in 1651: see his *Journal*, ed. Penney (1911), I, 1–12, 162.

[1] *Adventures by Sea of Edward Coxere*, ed. E. H. W. Meyerstein (1945), p. 89.

[2] Among many accounts of this group of writings two which may be found useful are in J. L. Lange, *Histoire de l'internationalisme*, I (1919), to 1648 and K. von Raumer, *Ewiger Friede* (1953).

freedom to fight for their own hands was to be obtained by a crusade against Islam. The idea of a Europe united in such a cause went back to the Middle Ages, and it was akin to what the Greeks and Romans thought of the barbarians. It had often been invoked in the sixteenth century, but even then it had been in no way related to political realities; it survived not merely into the seventeenth, but all the way through it. In 1672 the chief minister of the elector of Mainz sent Gottfried Wilhelm Leibniz, then twenty-six years old, to submit his Consilium Aegyptiacum to the pacific and reasonable minister, Pomponne, in Paris. Leibniz, so famous afterwards in many directions, and among others as an advocate of Christian reunion, is sometimes praised for this scheme. It invited Louis XIV to turn from his intention of invading Holland and use his arms against the Holland of the East. Pomponne, indeed, wrote urbanely to the General Feuquières:[1] 'Je ne vous dis rien sur les projets d'une guerre sainte; mais vous savez qu'ils ont cessé d'être à la mode depuis St Louis.' But the main intention of the plan was to further the Mainz policy of co-operation between France and the Empire; it was offered as a more effective way of damaging the Dutch and their commerce, and, in any case, the crusading idea was itself a bellicose idea.[2] Long afterwards, when Leibniz as an old man wrote to the abbé de Saint Pierre about the abbé's plan for perpetual peace, he thought that there would be great difficulties, however it was attempted, but 'aider l'empereur a chasser le Turc de l'Europe serait peut-être le moyen de venir à bout de ce mal'.[3]

[1] This was Isaac Pas, the father of the Feuquières mentioned on p. 92 below.
[2] *Die Werke von Leibniz*, ed. O. Klopp, 1e Reihe, II (1864), xxxiii.
[3] 'Lettre à Mr L'Abbé de S. Pierre', in *Opera Omnia* (1763), IV, 61 ff., dated 7 February 1715.

There were, as I have said, exceptions to this retention of war in the projects for perpetual peace, and the most interesting of them is afforded by that mysterious work the *Nouveau Cynée* of Emeric Crucé. The author is mysterious. His correct French name seems to have been satisfactorily established within the last century; but no one knows when he was born or how he made his living. The book is mysterious: although there were two editions, in 1623 and 1624, less than a dozen copies of the two are known to exist.[1] It is a project for an association of monarchs and republics with a standing assembly in Venice, but it has the surprising feature that the Turkish sultan is to be not merely included but given the first place in precedence. If there is an intentional paradox here, that cannot be said of some of the other proposals or the arguments advanced for them. Toleration, the sciences and various internal reforms for France are treated with a rationalistic radicalism which strikes many readers as oddly anticipatory of the eighteenth-century enlightenment. Recent studies of the libertine writers of early seventeenth-century France have, indeed, taught us that there was a formed and coherent rationalist and critical tendency in Crucé's time,[2] and none of his ideas is unique; but the combination of so many in his rapid argument gives his book a character of its own.

Even so it was not fundamentally more illuminating than the other internationalist Utopias. Its inclusion of the Turks

---

[1] I have used the edition, with English translation, of T. W. Balch (1909). Leibniz saw the book as a young man, but in his old age he could not lay hands on his copy.

[2] In our discussions at Belfast, Professor Lough mentioned the example of Cyrano de Bergerac, who anticipated a famous jibe against war in Voltaire's *Micromégas*.

marks emancipation from the crusading tradition; but the Turks were habitual allies of the French and even this is not universalism. There was living in Paris when Crucé published it another writer who had already worked out in various books truly universal doctrines of international relations, grounded in the belief that natural law binds the whole of mankind together in a community by ties of obligation and right. It is possible that Crucé knew this man, Hugo Grotius, whose treatise *De jure belli ac pacis* appeared in 1625.[1]

The projects for peace which did not envisage truly universal peace carried on one of the simple, leading ideas about war which the century inherited, one which is still common, a classification of wars into three kinds. War between States was distinguished from civil war, as it had been when the Romans used the words 'bellum civile', and everybody thought that civil war, 'blood against blood, self against self',[2] was the more dreadful of the two. On the other hand, the third type, war against the infidel, had its own high justification. In comparison with it, war between Christian kings was itself a kind of civil war: Shakespeare made one such king say

> I always thought
> It was both impious and unnatural
> That such immanity and bloody strife
> Should reign among professors of one faith.[3]

---

[1] This possibility becomes a probability if we accept the skilful reasoning of A. Saitta, 'Un riformatore pacifista contemporaneo del Richelieu: E. Crucé', in *Rivista storica italiana*, LXIII (1951), 180 ff., which shows that Crucé may have been on the fringe of the associates of Father Joseph.

[2] *King Richard the Third*, II, iv.

[3] *King Henry the Sixth, First Part*, v, i. For other references to Shakespeare see the essay, 'Shakespeare on the Wars of England', in J. Laird's *Philosophical Incursions into English Literature* (1946), which is none the less useful for its

This classification of wars embodied a number of distinctions which were evidently real. There were contrasts in the character of the fighting. Civil war involved irregular, undisciplined forces; not subject to the laws of war, such as they were, and this made it hard for either to treat the other as a 'loyal foe'. War against the Turks was not war against an uncivilized enemy, but it was outside the usages which the countries of western and central Europe had built up in terms of chivalry and law. Further afield, in Indonesia or even in North Africa, war against Islam became mere mutual butchery, like the worst wars with the heathens of America. There was a similar contrast from the technical military point of view. The armies of the European states-system were by no means all alike; but in armament, organization and discipline they had at least as much in common as the societies to which they belonged, and they were totally unlike their opponents.

The threefold division of wars was, however, unsatisfactory. The differences between civil and foreign war did not bulk as large for professional soldiers as it did for lawyers or patriotic spectators; still less did it for the Huguenot leaders in France, for instance, or for the foreign allies who came to their assistance. Sometimes it was difficult to draw a line between civil and regular war. There was no great difference in their ultimate social character between those of the wars within England, Scotland and Ireland from 1640 to 1651 which were civil wars and those of them which were officially wars between the kingdoms. The Thirty Years War was

purpose because its writer did not go behind Shakespeare to his sources. P. A. Jorgensen's *Shakespeare's Military World* (1955) has a wider scope and interesting discussions.

a succession of official wars between States, and yet there were poets and also lawyers who deplored it as a civil war within the German nation.[1]

Even if there had been no such border-line cases, and there were many, the tidy tripartite classification of wars ignored one cardinal fact. Wars of each type easily turned into war of either of the other kinds. Civil war was often a sequel to external victory. It always had been so, and the Greek and Roman historians showed it clearly. Thucydides showed how the victories of Sparta and Athens over the Persians led on to their internecine strife in the Peloponnesian War; Plutarch, how the legions of Sulla returned from Asia to march against the gates of Rome; Caesar himself, how he came to cross the Rubicon. The great Condé returned to France from his victories over Spain to fight in the civil war of the Fronde. Still more obviously, civil war was often a consequence of external defeat. If Buckingham had relieved la Rochelle, we might never have heard of Oliver Cromwell. Nothing is more familiar in history than the breaking-up of alliances which have been held together by a common purpose in war but become separate or warring elements when the pressure of common necessity relaxes. It is not only alliances that dissolve when peace comes; the same thing sometimes happens to the closer unity of single or multiple States. When the peace of le Cateau Cambrésis in 1559 interrupted a long succession of wars between France and Spain, there followed on the one side the French wars of religion and on the other the Netherlands revolt against

[1] In paragraphs CXIX–CXXI of the last dissertation in his *De jure naturae et gentium dissertationes* (1676), Samuel Rachel advocated a system of 'collective security' for Europe and, failing that, resistance to the tendency of the Holy Roman Empire to split into separate sovereignties.

Spain. By 1635 these contentions with others were again gathered into a general international war with France on one side and Spain on the other; but in 1648, when the Thirty Years War petered out, Europe was again in a phase of civil warfare, which has been summed up in the phrase, 'Six Contemporaneous Revolutions'.[1] There was a continuous rhythmic movement in which predominantly international wars alternated with predominantly civil wars. But, more often than not, the wars which were predominantly of one class had also some of the characteristics of the other.

Except from the legal and constitutional point of view there was, in fact, no clear distinction between civil war and external war. Some unorganized rabble might break into desperate revolt and challenge the constituted forces of order; they might have to improvise almost everything that was military; but even in the most unpremeditated outbreaks there were some veteran soldiers, some weapons in store, some notions of discipline and tactics. Whenever the contest deserved the name of civil war there was much more. The Huguenots possessed almost all the notes of a regular political community; they had their guaranteed constitutional liberties, their troops, their fortresses, their trained commanders of every rank up to the highest. The Catalans who fought against their Castilian king had everything that constituted a State except the crowned head. The Roundheads in the English civil war were not all peaceable civilians. The whole English people were liable for some sort of training in the militia and, even if they were obsolete, every

[1] This is the title of a useful book by the late R. B. Merriman (1938). The same writer's publication of 1937 with the same title is a reprinted lecture covering the same ground more briefly.

county had its stock of weapons and armour. Early in the reign of Charles I, the boys at Lincoln Grammar School did military drill under 'an old Low-Country soldier',[1] and at Edgehill the royal troops had to face not a few officers who had served under Gustavus or Frederick Henry of Orange. The rebels won, partly because they had the navy on their side. It happened repeatedly that in the initial stages of a civil war neither side treated the other as having any of the rights of belligerents, but, as it went on, they both came to apply the accepted rules to prisoners, to flags of truce and to their enemies' proceedings in general. Even civil war was not merely an aberration but a part of the regular institution of war.

If for our purpose we ought to look beyond the distinction between normal warfare and civil warfare, the same holds good of the distinction between wars within Western civilization and wars on its frontiers. No kind of war in which Europeans engaged was external to European civilization. The armies and the military monarchies which grew up in the long struggle against the Turks had much to do with the consolidation of the military element in European institutions and with the persistence of wars within Europe. Even the wars of colonization and distant conquest contributed to the same results and so did the subsequent colonial wars between Europeans. For about the first half of the seventeenth century it was commonly believed that two European powers could be at war outside Europe and at peace within it. There was fierce rivalry on and beyond the Eastern and Western seas between the three Atlantic maritime powers, the Portuguese, the Dutch and the English. The

[1] Lucy Hutchinson, *Life of Colonel Hutchinson*, ed. Firth (1885), I, 70-1.

quarrels of the great trading companies, with indigenous princes as their allies, deserved the name of wars for many years before the States were involved in Europe. Governments were slow to take up the merchants' quarrels. For many years they gave diplomatic support and rendered underhand assistance by lending ships and supplying arms; but they only allowed active operations to go on, for instance, in Brazil and the Spice Islands, as private enterprises. In the end they failed to localize these wars. The quarrel of the English and the Dutch, like the quarrel of the Dutch and the Portuguese, came to a head in regular European hostilities. At a later date the scuffles of French and English fur-traders around Hudson Bay were likewise subsumed into the war of Louis XIV. Economic and colonizing rivalries overseas took a place in the antecedents of European fighting. Distant wars could not be held at arm's length for ever. War beyond the confines of European civilization recoiled and became—became, not merely engendered—war within them, just as war between States became civil war. Nor could war near at hand always be hemmed in. Civil combatants summoned foreign aid and kindled international wars; international wars in Europe prepared the way to pitting the Iroquois against their neighbours and the sultan of Ternate against the islanders of Tidore. The three species all belonged to the institution of war and they were closely interlocked.

Seventeenth-century writers, with a partial exception which I shall mention in a moment, took a rationalist view of war. Authoritarian writers saw, always in the same hands, the maintenance of order, which was a necessary condition of justice, and defence against external enemies, which was a necessary condition of order. They recognized that the defender might be tempted to become an aggressor, and they counselled him to overcome the temptation.[1] But they regarded these three things, police, defence and aggression, as within the scope of his purpose and will, and the elements of disorder and the foreign enemies as the recalcitrant subject-matter over which that sovereign will had to be asserted.

One expression of this way of thinking is the doctrine of Clausewitz that war is 'a continuation of policy by other means'. Clausewitz used the language of a later age, but this rationalist view of war is very old, far older than the seventeenth-century maxim that war is 'ratio ultima regum'.[2] If, however, we read the statements of their aims at the inception of their wars either in the public proclamations or in the confidential correspondence of statesmen and then compare them with the aims they actually prosecuted at successive stages of the wars, we see that, as soon as war began and an enemy opposed his resistance to their policy, it always became impossible to continue it unaltered; it had to be modified to suit new conditions. The enemy narrowed down the field of the possible; allies exacted concessions that were incompatible with the original purposes, and neutrals took advantage of their opportunities. The statesmen themselves found their policy superseded, perhaps by something more modest, perhaps by something more ambitious, always by something new. War created policy rather than

[1] In this Fénelon was like them. In his *Télémaque* (1699) he pleaded powerfully for peace and reason in the relations of States, but his plan took the form of good advice to his royal pupil. In this he retained the common view expressed, for instance, in Racine's *Athalie*, iv, iii; v, viii.

[2] This phrase 'was probably originated by Richelieu or in his circle', J. Evelyn, *Diary*, ed. E. S. de Beer, ii (1956), 125, n. 4.

continued it. It was not under the control of the statesmen; it shifted their relation, not only to the forces of other States, but to those within their own States. Only very violent events could displace a monarch, but it seldom happened that the minister who enunciated the aims of a war when it began was still pursuing them or still in office when it ended.

I said there was an exception, if a partial exception, to this. It is the exception of the many political writers in the seventeenth century who did not accept the simple view of the State as a machinery of authority and obedience, or divine right and loyalty. They maintained in their different ways that the consent of the governed was essential to the nature of good government or even of government itself, or that in some way law and not men, not individual or even collective will, ought to rule. All of them insisted that political organization ought to be regarded from the point of view of the community which is organized. Their predecessors in the sixteenth century, whose books they read and reprinted, had elaborated their own versions of the social contract theory, which for them was more than an analysis of the political community, or a theory by which due account could be paid both to consent and to obedience. It implied that a body of men voluntarily entering into a social contract might be entitled to act as a political community, whatever prior rights might be claimed by kings or republican governments whom they found in territorial possession. In the confusion of the later sixteenth century, voluntary political associations actually did assert pretensions which were incompatible with the sovereignty of the existing rulers. In the seventeenth the Scottish National Covenant of 1638 did so, and also the Catholic Confederacy and oath of association in

Ireland in 1642. Such a plan was proposed by the English Whigs in 1678, in 1688, and perhaps in 1714. These associations either waged war or were willing to wage it. The political theories which justify them show that the liberal thinkers of the seventeenth century also paid little or no regard to the distinction between civil war and war between States. But they did not go further and treat the States as having in their international relations this character of voluntary association. If they had done so, the results might have been illuminating; but as it was the liberal writers scarcely departed from the rationalist view of international war.

It was in the seventeenth century that historians began to treat the history of Europe in the way that is still common, as an aggregate of the histories of different countries. In English this was perhaps first practised by Edward Grimeston, an industrious translator who published volumes on the histories of France, Spain, the Low Countries, the Empire, and Turkey, here and there omitting something from his original and referring the reader to 'that countrie historie'.[1] This was an improvement in the lay-out of European histories at a time when a number of States were growing stronger and the important transactions of politics were becoming concentrated in their hands. It did, however, further the assumption that international affairs were regulated by the wills of these separate States, much as the authoritarian thinkers believed that the domestic history of States was regulated by the wills of their masters. The history of European wars can, indeed, be written in terms of diplomatic correspondence, declarations of war, hostilities, peace

[1] See Appendix, no. 4.

conferences and treaties; but behind all these rational processes was something much more complicated. In a dispatch from Algiers in 1681 a British admiral wrote: 'I am very confident that His Majesty hath been twice, if not thrice, engaged in a war with these people by the misbehaviour of his consuls.'[1] In an article on the Anglo-Scottish border, I read: 'reiving and rapine can frequently not be separated neatly into international and domestic incidents.'[2] The imperial general, Raimondo Montecuccoli, was not thinking only of the regions fronting the Turks, when he wrote in 1668 that within living memory in his part of the world there had been no peace that was real and not slippery or suspect. What appeared so clearly on the frontiers of Europe was always latent and sometimes manifest within them. The distinction between war and peace was no easier to draw than that between civil war and international war. To declare war was not only a preliminary to the authorized operations of fleets and armies; it was letting loose the dogs of war. To sign an armistice was sometimes not merely registering a decision, but giving in to something that thousands of people had brought about. War was an activity which States controlled, so far as they were able, in its outbreak and conduct and termination; but it was much more than an activity of States. To understand what it was we must shake ourselves free of the modern dictionary definition of war as 'hostile contention by means of armed forces carried on by nations, states or rulers or between parties in

---

[1] See below, p. 124.
[2] D. Hay, in *Dumfriesshire and Galloway Natural History and Antiquarian Soc. Trans.* (3rd ser.), XXXI (1954), 147. This article deals with an earlier period, but the remark is true of the whole history of this frontier, down to its disappearance in 1603.

the same nation or state'.[1] Fifty-five years after Grotius published his great book, another legal writer took him to task for having followed too closely the definition of Cicero, who called it simply, 'contending by force', 'certatio per vim'. The jurist, he thought, must exclude from his consideration private wars and mixed wars; only public wars are his concern.[2] But this was to attack only part of a problem which Grotius rightly treated as a whole. My first conclusion was that war was an institution. My second is that it cannot be understood except as part of a general mêlée. If there seems to be some contradiction between these two conclusions, perhaps it may be resolved by the third.

[1] *The Concise Oxford Dictionary* (1911).
[2] J. W. Textor, *Synopsis juris gentium* (1690), p. 149.

CHAPTER II

THE ANALOGY OF THE DUEL

THROUGHOUT history statesmen have asserted the power of their States against competing powers, whether these have been other States or barbarian hordes, or dissident forces within their own borders. In some societies they have repressed the blood-feuds between tribes or families, in some the feudal turbulence of over-mighty subjects, in some the depredations of bandits, in some the stirrings of the populace, in some the mutinies of soldiers or the challenges of generals. Sometimes the statesmen have acted defensively; and sometimes they have taken the initiative; but in either case they have borne the responsibility of keeping or restoring the peace, and therefore they have tried, according to the possibilities of their times, to acquire a monopoly of force. In the seventeenth century, in the great territorial States of Europe, domestic peace was the King's peace, and so we find the principle stated 'le roi seul a droit de glaive'.[1] These words are taken from the

---

[1] Preamble to the Decree of 26 June 1599 (J. Savaron, *Traicte contre les duels* (1610), p. 79). This decree is not given in A. J. L. Jourdan, Decrusy and Isambert, *Recueil des anciens lois françaises*, 29 vols. (1822–33). In spite of this and other omissions, the index to the *Recueil* will be found useful. In J. J. S. Wharton, *Law Lexicon* (1848), *ius gladii* is defined as 'the executory power of the sovereign'. I have not found any seventeenth-century example of this usage, and I do not know whether the phrase in the Decree is taken from any system of jurisprudence. Du Cange, *Lexicon* (ed. Henschel, IV, 1885), gives a number of earlier instances from which it can be seen how the phrase came to be used. Seventeenth-century legal and political writers frequently quoted St Paul's words about the ruler (*potestas*) in Rom. xiii. 4, 'non enim sine causa gladium portat'. For the general nature of the right to use force see W. Platzhoff,

preamble of a French royal decree against duelling. In more countries than one it was a task of the State to put this practice down. This part of the endless history of the assertion of State power in the interests of peace[1] shows clearly in miniature some features of physical and moral force which are also present on an enormously larger scale in the social history of war, where they are much more difficult to discern because of the innumerable social factors involved in war. It will therefore give indications which may be used in mapping that larger area. It has, indeed, sometimes been appealed to as if simple conclusions could be drawn from duelling and applied straight away to war. A number of writers, more particularly supporters of plans for universal peace, have thought that the suppression of duelling was a straightforward operation, successfully accomplished by intelligent action, which, given only courage and common sense, could be repeated on an international scale.

The particular kind of duelling with which we are concerned is the private duel between a challenger and one who accepts his challenge. It was distinguished from a mere fight or encounter by being fought at a time and place agreed upon beforehand, with weapons chosen by the acceptor. It was also quite distinct from the judicial duel of the Middle Ages, of which the last traces disappeared from most of Europe before 1600. Seventeenth-century writers did not always draw this distinction clearly; in their anxiety to dis-

Die Theorie von der Mordbefügnis der Obrigkeit im XVI Jahrhundert, Historische Studien (1906), which shows that there were many survivals in the seventeenth century of the view that *raison d'état* justified killing without process of law.

[1] Crucé, *Nouveau Cynée*, 113–24, deals with duelling as one of the evils which could be overcome if his main plan was adopted.

credit duelling as uncivilized some of them insisted that the judicial combat came in with the barbarian invaders of the Roman empire. As the private duel was partly derived from the judicial duel it was not unfair to affix this stigma to it, but, besides the main difference that judicial duels were part of a system, if a primitive and clumsy system, of law, there were other easily visible differences. Trials by wager of battle required umpires and attendant officials and they were fought before spectators. Some of them, when the umpires were kings, were amongst the greatest spectacles of the declining days of chivalry; such was the combat of Hereford and Norfolk which we know from Shakespeare's *Richard II* or the day of the *coup de Jarnac* before Henry II of France. It was very seldom that private duels were fought where they could be seen. There was a curious case in 1683 of a meeting of three with three in St James's Square in London, when half the combatants were killed and two more were seriously wounded; but that was altogether exceptional. For the most part there was a conventional half-concealment. In London, for instance, everyone knew that Southampton Fields was a regular resort for duellists, but nothing was done to stop up their access to the place.

This kind of duelling is familiar to most of us if not in history or memoirs or diaries then in fiction. Apart from rare exceptions the opponents fought on foot and with swords. In the seventeenth century they fought to kill.[1] To the popular imagination such a duel appears picturesque and chivalrous. A historian will see little that is picturesque. If any

---

[1] This may be partly due to the use of the small-sword, which was fashionable in England from the Restoration, but came in earlier on the Continent. As a thrusting weapon it was more lethal than the long rapier for both cut and thrust. See J. D. Aylward, *The Small-Sword in England* (*s.a.* 1946).

seventeenth-century painters took duels as their subjects they were few, and what they saw was not an elegant, if dangerous, fencing bout between athletic young men, but a furtive and bloody fight. Romance has built up its fiction on the basis of the strict rules of courtesy which were supposed to regulate the fighting, and the chivalrous motives that were supposed to induce it: 'for he had spoken lightly of a woman's name', 'pistols for two, coffee for one', and so on. There was something to build this on. According to one strict definition of sport, there was a sporting element in the duel: it was a match, contested at a fixed place and time, sometimes on a marked-out ground (a τέμενος or sacred enclosure), and according to rules.[1] There were cool customers who addressed themselves to it in a cultivated and easy manner, and there were some generous duellists who never intended to do more than disarm their opponents. But viewed fairly and as a whole the historical reality was not pretty. Sometimes the rules were broken: John Law the financier killed 'Beau Wilson' unfairly,[2] and there were many occasions when courts of law had to decide whether they were dealing with set duels or murderous assaults. In the seventeenth century the seconds frequently fought as well as the principals: Montaigne, whose *Essays* were still widely read, condemned this custom, which was new in his time, as cowardly,[3] but it still went on. There were men of standing and principle who engaged in duels, but the known duellists were often 'Hectors', repulsive bullies, questionable hangers-on of rank and fashion. There is a description

[1] J. Huizinga, *Homo Ludens* (1940) in *Gezamelde Werken*, v (1950), 21–2.
[2] John Evelyn, *Diary* (1694), ed. E. S. de Beer, v, 175–6.
[3] Bk. II, c. xxvii.

of a French duellist named Bouteville which frightfully resembles what we know of modern gangsters.[1] There were few places of great resort without great quarrellers who carried themselves insolently and imperiously.[2] There were professional seconds who took fees for their services irrespective of the cause; in London they were called 'free-willers'.[3] When the lives of the combatants are traced they are often found to have been before or afterwards plain criminals or madmen.

If the romantic picture of the fighting is mainly imaginary, the same is true of the causes of the quarrel. It is, indeed, the distinctive feature of this kind of duel that it was connected with the point of honour; it is sometimes distinguished from the judicial or the chivalric duel as the 'duel of honour'. Honour demanded that insults should be avenged, especially the supreme insult of formally giving the lie. The laws of honour were elaborately codified. The code was worked out and discussed in many books, some of them pedantic and tedious, but others learned and well written. The best of them had an international circulation and authority. The code had remote and complex origins, but as a formal body of doctrine it belonged primarily to sixteenth-century Italy, and it was there that its most famous masters wrote.[4] They were not eccentrics or writers of a literary underworld; they dedicated their books to kings and princes, and statesmen

---

[1] Quoted by P. Rocques in his preliminary discourse to J. Basnage, *Dissertation historique du duel* (ed. 1740).

[2] J. Hales, *Golden Remains* (1658), p. 110.

[3] Bodl. MS. Rawl. D 8, p. 53, and in the index under Sir Thomas Armstrong, 1659.

[4] F. R. Bryson, *The Point of Honor in Sixteenth-Century Italy* (1935) and *The Sixteenth Century Italian Duel* (1938) are useful summaries of the literature with full references.

read them. In 1558 G. B. Possevino's *Dialogo dell' honore* of 1556 was reprinted with his brother Antonio's *Trattato*. The first is dedicated to the Cardinal di Santo Fiore and the second to the duke of Savoy. The Bodleian has Sir Christopher Hatton's autographed copy, and his autograph also appears twice on a manuscript translation, dedicated to him, of Paris de Puteo's *Duello*.[1] We must be prepared to believe that there were many occasions on which two honourable men, each, as he thought, in the right, found themselves in a predicament from which the only exit was a fight to the death. More than one man is known to have said as he was dying that the man who had killed him was still his best friend. Sometimes, when a man was killed, his family and friends felt no more resentment than if he had broken his neck in the hunting field. We cannot tell whether it was often so, or whether it was often nearly so. But we do know that it was sometimes not like this at all. A plain-spoken preacher in the reign of James I said: '*Drinking, Gameing and Whores*, these are the rotten bones that lie hid under this painted *Sepulchre* and title of *Honour*.' The greatest part of challenges for some time past, according to this preacher, had been in taverns, drinking houses and stews.[2] At the end of the century another English divine could write that duelling was chiefly in wicked and infamous company.[3] There may have been duels fought to punish slanders on innocent ladies; we know that there were some that started with cheating at cards.

If this were a contemporary problem we should approach

---

[1] See E. A. Strathmann in *Times Literary Supplement*, 13 April 1956, p. 228.
[2] J. Hales, *Golden Remains* (1659), p. 113.
[3] T. Comber, *Discourse of Duels* (1687), p. 52.

it by way of statistics. So far as I know no one has attempted that, and yet, though it might not be worth while to search and check every available outlying source of information, it would be valuable to go through at any rate the more accessible and to arrange from year to year for each country the number of recorded duels, the number of fatal and other casualties, the number of prosecutions and convictions, and whatever other particulars can be treated numerically. Unless and until this is done much must remain uncertain. It may be that duelling was not general, but occurred sporadically both in a social and geographical sense. There seems to be more evidence of it in Italy, France, Spain, England and Sweden than elsewhere. It may have been characteristic of city life rather than of the countryside. But it would be unreasonable to doubt that it was a serious evil. Provisionally we may accept the statement, which was made by more than one writer of the time, that in the first years of the century few or none of the noble families of France had escaped losses of life from this custom.[1]

Duelling, in the words of an English proclamation,[2] deprived the State of strong limbs and therefore its decline was due to State policy and was first and foremost 'an episode in the growth of the rule of law'.[3] This, however, does not mean merely that the States passed laws against duelling and enforced them. The process was much more complicated. In some respects it was adapted to the differing social con-

---

[1] Savaron, p. 49, is the best of these. Savaron was a political writer of some importance.

[2] Steele and Crawford, *Tudor and Stuart Proclamations*, no. 1143.

[3] Sir William Holdsworth, *History of English Law*, I (third ed. 1922), 579. This passage and others in vol. v (*s.a.*), 199–201, and vol. VII (*s.a.*), 356, I. 4, of the same work give an excellent account of the English law in the matter.

ditions of the various countries, but most of its elements seem to be present to some degree everywhere; there are coincidences of dates between the enactments in different countries; indeed, there was something like an international movement against duelling. The laws of one country were imitated abroad; the successes of one were held up as an example for imitation in others. At the beginning of the seventeenth century there were already many legal prohibitions of duelling as such; but, in order to make them effective, the stronger States followed two lines of reform. They decided, in what is nearly always the right sense, a question which faces the opponents of all great social evils, the question whether simply to aim at abolition or to aim at it through amelioration. Assuming that men would want to fight duels, they provided an alternative procedure for working off the passions that provoked them. In France King Henry IV reintroduced the judicial duel in 1609, and, although this revival was short-lived, the severe repression of Richelieu and Louis XIV retained the principle that quarrels likely to lead to duels must be submitted not to the ordinary courts of law but to a specially constituted and more appropriate body, the *tribunal des maréchaux*.

In England, King James I worked out a plan against duelling with the help of the ablest of his councillors. Sir Edward Coke drew up a statement of the existing law regarding revenge, slander, self-defence and private duel. By common law it was already murder to kill a man in duel; but there were no laws against the sending or accepting of challenges, nor against acting as seconds or other contributory acts. These were now forbidden by proclamations, and the main proclamation was published with a supporting argument in a pamphlet of 119 pages.[1] Bacon, when he became attorney-general in 1613, found that there had recently been six notorious quarrels in high places: one had been quenched by the king, but one had been fatally fought out and two were reported to have been fought out overseas. He surveyed the problem like a true statesman. 'First,' he wrote to the king, 'I consider that the offence hath vogue only amongst noble persons or persons of quality.' Such were to be proceeded against in the Star Chamber, and in his charge there, when two parties were prosecuted for sending and accepting a challenge, Bacon said: 'We have not to do in this case, so much with particular persons as with unsound and depraved opinions, like the dominations and spirits of the air which the Scripture speaketh of.'[2] He used the Star Chamber more than once to good purpose; but a generation later it was abolished. The same fate overtook another court, the court of the marshal, to which King James assigned the function of composing the disputes which would lead to duels. In 1640 John Pym said in parliament that this court was arbitrary. Suitable legal objections to it were easily found, and it ceased to act.[3] In 1668 the College of Arms promoted a bill which according to the preamble, was intended to suppress duelling. Among other things, it would have given the earl marshal and other commissioners power to decide disputes over place and precedence and

[1] *A publication of His Majesties Edict and Severe Censure against Private Combats and Combatants* (1613).

[2] *The Works of Francis Bacon*, ed. J. Spedding, XI, *The Letters and Life*, IV (1868), 396–409; VI (1872), 103ff.; J. Gutch, *Collectanea Curiosa*, I (1781), 9–12; the statement about the Turks on p. 404 comes from the third Letter dated 1 June 1560 in O. G. de Busbecq, *Legationis Turcicae Epistolae IV*.

[3] Sir Simonds D'Ewes, *Journal*, ed. W. Notestein, I (1923), 7 and 23 November 1640, 19 February 1640–1.

usurpations of arms. The bill mentions as one ground that these often led to duels: but the House of Commons did not want to allow the heralds in England such a legal right to fees as they have in Scotland and so the bill was thrown out.[1] The struggle against duelling had to be conducted in the ordinary courts of law. These courts did not only repress duelling, they tried to eliminate its causes. They provided legal satisfaction where men had been wont to seek satisfaction by fighting. To this end they built up the law against defamation. In a judgement of 1704 the great Lord Chief Justice Holt said: 'men's tongues growing more virulent, and irreparable damage arising from words, it has been by experience found, that unless men can get satisfaction by law, they will be apt to take it themselves', and so the law of slander was needed, and by that time it was already gradually diminishing the possibilities of provocation.

It was not only the central executive and judicial authorities who tried to repress the custom. There were communities within the community where duelling was specially likely and specially undesirable. The universities were full of excitable young men: in 1634 Archbishop Laud's statutes for Oxford prescribed penalties for sending or accepting a challenge or for fighting a duel; the Latin clause still stands in the current edition of the statutes.[2] But it was in armies that duels were most likely and most damaging. One after another in their articles of war the States or their commanders prohibited duelling, and the quarrels that led to it, and they provided alternative methods for settling

[1] For a summary of the bill see *Historical Manuscripts Commission, 8th Report*, 122, for a comment J. Millward, *Parliamentary Diary*, ed. Caroline Robbins (1938), p. 137.
[2] Stat. Tit. xv, 9. Other universities had similar rules, Uppsala in 1682.

them.[1] The Elector of Brandenburg's articles of 1688 were supposed to have been the best provisions.[2]

If the States and their armies, and the universities, tried to stamp the custom out, the churches, as was to be expected, were even more strongly against it. The Council of Trent had forbidden the practice sternly enough;[3] two sixteenth-century popes had extended these prohibitions to cover further related offences;[4] the best of all the books against duelling, Scipione Maffei, *Della scienza chiamata cavalleresca*, was dedicated in 1710 to Clement XI. In France the church-men backed up the efforts of the statesmen. Although he was a layman I may mention here Jean Chenel, Sieur de la Chapponaye, who published in 1617 his book *Les révélations de l'hermite solitaire* with preliminary sonnets to the king, each member of the royal family and the nobility collec-tively. He had been to Malta and to Italy, and this book describes, with engravings, his emblematical visions. He wanted to found a military religious order, in the first place for crusading, and he had already published its rules. One of them was that the members 'renonceront a tous duels et assassinats, et a toutes querelles hors le service du Roy', and Chapponaye offered to settle the question by single combat with a chosen champion of the duellists.[5] A more promising

---

[1] See the collection of such codes in the widely used *Corpus juris militaris*. The British Museum has an edition of 1674 which is catalogued under the name of the editor, Petrus Pappus von Tratzburg.

[2] Maffei, *Della scienza chiamata cavalleresca*, p. 344.

[3] Sess. 25, de Reformatione, Can. 19.   [4] Gregory XIII and Clement VIII.

[5] I have not seen the original issue of the rules, separately printed at Nantes in 1614. As the book of 1617 is rare, I quote the following lines from the commendatory sonnet by Le Roy, who writes that God

> Promet à vos désirs que depuis le Bosphore
> Iusqu'aux derniers confins des terres de l'Aurore
> Vous ferez une mer du sang des Circoncis.

attempt to engage the nobles against duelling on religious grounds was initiated in 1651, the year of one of the edicts issued in the minority of Louis XIV. At the instance of Jean-Jacques Olier, the founder of the Sulpician congregation, an association was formed and its members used their influence with the nobility of their provinces.[1]

There was nothing in this matter to distinguish the attitude of Protestant from that of Catholic divines. One after another through the century English preachers and theologians of every colour denounced the custom, the 'ever memorable' John Hales,[2] John Donne,[3] Thomas Fuller,[4] Joseph Hall,[5] Jeremy Taylor,[6] Gilbert Burnet,[7] Jeremy Collier.[8] The form of their pleas changed with the changes of literary fashion. Their arguments changed with the prevailing habits of thought. At the beginning of the century it was necessary to explain that when Cain said, as the Septuagint has it, 'Let us go into the field', Abel 'understood it not as a Challenge'. At the end it was more effective to insist on the advantages of respect for law, which is a guarantee, amongst other things, against attacks on property by 'the under-sort of People'.[9] But it was never super-

---

[1] I have also not seen Anatole, Marquis Granges de Surgeres, *Le duel et la noblesse de Languedoc* (1902), which deals with this incident.

[2] 'Sermon of Duels preach'd at the Hague' before Sir Dudley Carleton, between 1616 and 1619, in *Golden Remains* (1659).

[3] Xmas Day 1622 in *LXXX Sermons* (1640), p. 5.

[4] *The Holy State* (1642), pp. 122 ff.

[5] *Works*, III (1662), 801.

[6] *Ductor dubitantium* (1660), p. 113.

[7] *Sermon preached before the Queen*, 11 March 1693/4, p. 27; *Exposition of the Church Catechism* (1710), p. 164; *Own Time* (Bk. VII), where, reflecting on the duel in which the Duke of Hamilton and Lord Mohun killed one another in 1712, he sees 'little hope' of rooting duelling out.

[8] 'Upon duelling' in *Essays upon Several Moral Subjects* (1697).

[9] Collier, p. 40.

fluous to restate the stock examples from the Bible, the classics and history; it was never difficult to prove that duelling was unchristian.

Outside the circle of divines it was not only Christian moralists like Locke[1] who stood on the same side; along with them were Lord Herbert of Cherbury,[2] Pierre Bayle,[3] and, partly following him, Bernard Mandeville;[4] the weight of opinion was overwhelming. With what result? It appears that there were only two countries in Europe of which we can say with any confidence that duelling was effectively brought under control in the seventeenth century. One country was France. Not only French writers, who may have had a motive for flattering the authorities, but also those of Italy[5] and England[6] treated it as a matter of common knowledge that this had been accomplished during the reign of Louis XIV. There are also references to the Dutch republic as a country where the laws were enforced; perhaps they had never been so badly needed there as in the monarchical countries. The Dutch enforced the death penalty for killing in duels in the East Indies.[7] Elsewhere, however, astonish-

---

[1] *Essay*, II, xxvii, 15, an incidental allusion. In his *Thoughts concerning Education* (1693), para. 199, Locke showed that a knowledge of fencing made young men more touchy and apt to engage in duels, but, recognizing that it was expected of a gentleman, left it to the discretion of fathers whether their sons should learn it.

[2] *Autobiography*.

[3] *Pensées diverses sur la comète* (1683).

[4] *The Fable of the Bees* (1714), Remark, R., ed. F. B. Kaye (1924), I, 198–223 and II, 91–6. Mandeville is perhaps also influenced by Hobbes whose views are in *Leviathan* (1651), pt. I, c. 10 and pt. II, c. 27.   [5] E.g. Maffei.

[6] Mandeville, *op. cit.* I, 94; E. Chambers, *Cyclopaedia* (1728), *s.v.* Duel; Addison in *Spectator*, no. 99. In the sixty-four years of Louis's reign there were only seven decrees, as against fourteen in the previous sixty-four years.

[7] See the case of the corporal who killed an Englishman at Cambello in a duel which lasted more than an hour, referred to on p. 137 of part II of no. 10 in the Appendix, below p. 152.

ingly little was accomplished. Not only were there still many duels, possibly—though we do not know—as many as ever. There was contempt of the laws against them. In parliamentary England there were duels over political quarrels.[1] King William III said, on a famous occasion, that if he had not been a king he would have challenged Lord Churchill, afterwards the great Duke of Marlborough. As a young man Churchill fought more than one duel; he issued a challenge when he had risen to the height of his career. He did more than connive at the escape of the master of Sinclair, who had been sentenced to death by a court-martial for an offence which was more like a double murder than duelling. He arranged for the criminal to return to the army in Prussian service.[2] A British officer might in theory be punished for accepting a challenge, he would be 'broke' if he refused it.[3] Each of the Portuguese garrisons in Ceylon had a spot a league or so away from the camp, some group of trees, where challenges and duels were permitted. No action was taken against a man who killed another in a duel at such a place, provided only that he absented himself from camp for eight days.[4] If this was so in armies, it was not less so among civilians. Duellists could avail themselves of perverted legal ingenuity, corrupt connivance among police and gaolers, help from bystanders, perjury by witnesses and pardons granted by favour. The mere quantity of the writings against duelling proves that it went on, and we

---

[1] See the *Dictionary of National Biography* under the names of Sir William Williams and Thomas, first Marquess of Wharton.

[2] See *Proceedings in the Court-Martial upon John, Master of Sinclair* (1828).

[3] Mandeville, *op. cit.* II, 95.

[4] C. R. Boxer in *Ceylon Historical Journal*, III (1953), 247. It does not appear that duelling was common either in Portugal itself or in Brazil.

know that in most parts of Europe and America it was not the seventeenth century nor the eighteenth but the nineteenth that saw it brought within its present narrow bounds.

How are we to account for the persistence of this custom which was so widely and so cogently condemned? It must, indeed, be admitted that arguments circulated openly in its favour. During the first half of the century many men still read the terse sentences in which Jean Bodin said that duelling must be tolerated lest worse evils broke in;[1] it was preferable to blood feuds and assassination by retainers or hired knaves. Bodin, indeed, was thinking of judicial duels, and at the end of the period, when the judicial duel had vanished, the jurists held that no duel was permissible when there could be any possible resort to law.[2] There were, however, ecclesiastics who devised excuses by which infractions of the Tridentine decree could be absolved; they would be forgotten now if it were not for the withering answer of Pascal in the seventh letter of the *Provincials*.[3] Here and there an isolated thinker might raise a fundamental doubt. John Selden, with his blunt and paradoxical common sense, said this in conversation: 'War is lawful, because God is the only judge betwixt two that are supreme.' And he continued 'Nay, what if we should bring it down, for argument's sake, to the sword-men? One gives me the lie ...the law has made no provision to give remedy for the injury...why am I not in this case supreme, and may then right myself?'[4]

---

[1] *De la république* (1577), bk. IV, c. viii.
[2] U. Huber, *De jure civitatis* (1713), p. 628.
[3] Published in 1656.
[4] *Table-Talk* (1892), pp. 59–60. This was said between 1634 and 1654.

The idea that there were two sides to the ethical question was perpetuated by the drama, especially by the French drama. Nothing could be better than a duel for providing excitement and suspense in a play. The best French dramatists thought it was not becoming, *bienséant*, for the fighting to take place openly on the stage, but that left open the opportunity for epigrammatic dialogue about it.[1] Molière expressed himself on the subject in at least five of his plays, and always came out unequivocally against the duel. Shakespeare did not object to sword-play, but no one can reasonably doubt that, at least in the character of Tybalt in *Romeo and Juliet*, he shows a distaste, a disdain, for the cruelty of duelling and the affectation that went with it. The position of Corneille is less clear. There are duels, if we include judicial duels, in eight of his plays; in some they are crucial incidents. The characters argue the case for and against, and some writers have thought that *Le Cid* was a defiance of Richelieu's policy of repression.[2] It seems, however, that they were mistaken. The most that can be conceded to them is that, although the official view always has the advantage, enough is said to satisfy its opponents among the audience.

There were such opponents, and if the open propaganda on their side did not amount to much, there was a good deal of indirect or incidental support for it. A modern reader who wades through the books against duelling cannot help wondering sometimes whether the writers were altogether

[1] For the French drama see the careful work of N. A. Bennetton, *The Social Significance of the Duel in Seventeenth-Century French Drama* (1938) which analyses references in about 145 plays, but is defective in arrangement and applies a very crude social doctrine.

[2] The most powerful expression of this view is in J. Michelet, *Histoire de France*, XII (1858), c. x, which ought not to be taken too seriously.

sincere in condemning the system when they interminably discussed the niceties of the laws of honour, such as who might challenge whom and how and on what occasions, and with what formalities a duel should be conducted. This doubt is raised, for instance, by the French lawyer and philosopher Scipion Dupleix who published his first edition in 1602 and his second in 1611, that is, after the severe edict of 1609.[1] A contemporary of his, Marc de la Béraudière, Seigneur de Mauvoisin and *chevalier de l'ordre du Roi*, describes himself as a simple soldier, and maintains that the only way to put down 'ceste miserable coustume' is for duels fought without the king's permission and after due efforts for a reconciliation to be forbidden on pain of death. Yet the last sentence of his rambling volume says that when a gentleman's mistress is insulted he ought to resent it and avenge the injury that has been done him.[2] It is one of the merits of Maffei's book that he exposes the deceptiveness of one class of writings against duels.[3] These are the manuals for composing differences. They set out from the assumption that all quarrels can be honourably settled without fighting; but their directions for negotiating and fulfilling

[1] *Les loix militaires touchant la duel.* The Bodleian copy of the first edition is imperfect, and so I have not been able to make a satisfactory comparison of the two.

[2] *Le combat de seul à seul en champ clos* (1608).

[3] This point is anticipated in a letter of 28 December 1575 from Cardinal Ferdinando de' Medici, afterwards grand duke of Tuscany, to the aged Girolamo Muzio, rebuking him for his criticism of the cardinal's manner of making peace between two Florentine gentlemen: S. Bongi, *Annali de Gabriel Giolito de' Ferrari*, I (1890), 307–9. Giolito was the Venetian printer who, with his brothers, published Muzio's book *Il duello*, dedicated to Emmanuel Philibert of Savoy, with privileges of Pope Julius II and the Venetian senate. There was a Spanish translation in 1552, and many Italian editions down to and after 1585. At the age of 81 Muzio was a professional expert on honour and the cardinal refers to 'la passione che vi preme di vedervi guastar la bottega'.

the terms of these settlements are so elaborate, so qualified and so easily infringed that in the upshot they merely magnify the importance of every trifle connected with the notions of honour and chivalry so as to make quarrels easier to pick, harder to end and altogether less repugnant.[1]

These ambiguities, where the moral issue seems so simple, bring us nearer to the heart of the problem of the survival of duelling. Strong forces pulled against the teachings of reason and humanity. Duelling and the notions of honour were closely knit with the pride and the fighting qualities of the governing classes, and no one doubted that these were needed by the State. A bitter opponent of duelling wrote: 'It's a maxim amongst such packed Jurors that such persons Offenders may in time repent and be useful unto the Nation';[2] and something like this was accepted by people of very different standing from partial jurymen. There is an example in Clarendon's *History of the Great Rebellion*,[3] and it is the more striking because Clarendon was the embodiment of the law-abiding spirit. Lord Grandison was wounded at the taking of Bristol in 1643 and carried to Jesus College, Oxford, where he died. In his eulogy on Grandison, Clarendon wrote that he was 'of that rare piety and devotion that the court could not show a more faultless person, or to whose example young men might more reasonably conform themselves. His personal valour and courage of all kinds (for he had sometimes indulged so much

[1] A good specimen is G. B. Olevano, *Trattato...nel quale...vien posto...il modo*, etc. (1603).

[2] Bodl. Lib. MS. Rawl. D, 8, p. 2.

[3] Ed. Macray, III (1888), 115. Robert Ward 'gentleman and commander' included a chapter against duelling, which is merely a summary of James I's *Edict and Severe Censure*, and the text of Gustavus's Articles in his *Animadversions of Warre* (1639), but owned up to having fought in three duels (p. 102).

to the corrupt opinion of honour as to venture himself in duels,) was very eminent.' The Rev. Dr Comber in his library might ask 'why should it not be as truly dishonourable to be a Passionate Fool, as a Coward';[1] but there was a public opinion which he could not move. The Jansenist theologian Pierre Nicole wrote: 'Combien de gens s'allaient autrefois battre en duel en déplorant et condamnant cette misérable coutûme,[2] et se blâmant eux-mêmes de la suivre. Mais ils n'avoient pas pour cela la force de mépriser le jugement de ces fous, qui les eussent traités de lâches s'ils eussent obéis à la raison.'[3] His testimony is the more valuable because he makes this point only incidentally, to illustrate the effectiveness of human will to carry out the directions of reason. It is interesting that, although he wrote as early as 1671, he referred to duelling as if it were a thing of the past.

The code of honour, which was the intellectual groundwork of duelling, was not held to be binding on all men. It was the code of gentlemen and it had its place in the growth of the ideal which ascribed higher duties and responsibilities and dignity to their status. As has happened in many other conditions of society, certain things were permitted and others denied to these privileged persons only. There were injuries which a king could ignore because it was beneath him to feel affronted by anyone except another king. Peasants or artisans also might ignore them without shame; but persons of honour must defend their honour: for them to draw the sword for this cause was equivalent to self-defence. This is sometimes called an aristocratic code; but it

---

[1] *Discourse of Duels* (1687), p. 37.
[2] La Béraudière, it will be remembered, uses the same phrase.
[3] *Essais de morale*, traité 1, c. xi. I have used the edition of 1730.

was a matter of some doubt and dispute whether it applied to a wider or a narrower body and whether the line was to be drawn according to social status or whether other considerations came in. Writers who thought that merchants were exempt from it might regard them as social inferiors; those who thought that old men or very young men or scholars need not accept challenges and ought not to send them tended to restrict duelling to men of the sword, military men, among whom the *noblesse de l'épeé* were traditionally reckoned. It was the custom in most European countries for large numbers of the landed, official and professional men habitually to wear their swords when they walked abroad. In practice and probably in the common opinion it was all such men, and not only aristocrats in a narrow sense, who were obliged to be careful of the point of honour. There is even some reason to think that the code helped up the gentry of western Europe from their subordination to the nobility. Selden said 'A duke ought to fight with a gentleman',[1] and Vauvenargues, who was a marquis but a penniless and unimportant marquis, wrote: 'Le duel avait un bon côté, qui était de mettre un frein à l'insolence des grands; aussi, je m'étonne qu'ils n'aient pas encore trouvé le moyen de l'abolir entièrement.'[2]

However that may have been, there was a connexion between duelling and the social structure of those times. It is sometimes said that what did away with duelling was the rise of the bourgeoisie. Among the currents of opinion against it there certainly were some which can be fairly

[1] *Ubi supra.*
[2] Luc de Clapiers, Marquis de Vauvenargues, *Maximes et réflexions* (1746), no. 641.

48

described as bourgeois, at least in so far as the bourgeois is contrasted with the feudal or the aristocratic or the military. Some of the clergymen and lawyers no doubt were typically bourgeois, and so were some of the literary men. Molière, though he was a court dramatist, saw the courtiers as the citizens saw them.[1] But to make the decline of duelling merely an incident of a transition from feudalism to capitalism seems to simplify too much. Maffei was another marquis, a wealthy and successful man and a good soldier. He was one of hundreds whose names and work are known to us, and who were surrounded by thousands of whom we are justified in saying, although we perceive them dimly, that they came from a wide variety of social origins, as wide as the responsiveness to Christian or rational humanitarianism, which was by no means limited to the bourgeoisie or invented by the bourgeois mind. Another point to notice is that neither side seems to have derived any effective support from organized interests. There were some people whose livelihood depended partly on duelling. For the manufacturers of weapons this is true only in a very subordinate degree. Perhaps the people who came nearest to depending on it were the fencing masters, who were naturally more prominent then than now; but it was their pupils, not they, who kept the custom going. No one suggested that the fencing masters formed a sinister interest[2] capable of influencing the fashion.

---

[1] In his *Don Juan* (1665), III, 3, one of his characters says: 'c'est en quoi je trouve la condition d'un gentilhomme malheureuse...d'être asservi par les lois de l'honneur au dérèglement de la conduite d'autrui.'

[2] This phrase, usually thought to be characteristic of the Benthamite way of looking at things, is used by William Penn in his *Works*, II (1726), 846, in the project of perpetual peace dated 1693/4.

The element of rational discussion, though far weightier than the element of rationally calculated interest, worked as a slow transforming force, at first almost powerless against the inert mass of irrational prejudice and habit. The change worked through many channels, and any attempt to trace it must take into account the immense complexity of the processes by which large social changes came about even in those relatively undeveloped societies. The change in opinion was slow, and so was the change in practice. Step by step the laws of the State, the armies, and the churches were made clearer and more adequate to the complexities of the evil; they were enforced more effectively, and the worst abuses were stifled one after another, until, at the end of the period, against this type of competition, the statesmen could look forward to establishing their monopoly of force.

After this review, we may ask what can be learnt from the duel about the nature of war. There is obviously no simple parallel, the relation of the two is rather that duelling was a very small element in that mêlée of which wars were the largest components. The difference of scale was so great, there was such a disproportion between the numbers of people involved directly or indirectly, and between the degrees to which they were affected, that the appropriate parallel to duelling would not be war. It would be some obstinate but limited social evil like juvenile delinquency or road casualties. This difference does, however, fortify the point that war was fixed in the order of society. Duelling persisted in spite of the constant efforts of some of the most powerful and some of the most enlightened men, not only in their private but in their official and social capacities. They used all their resources against it, including those of social study and propaganda and practical inventiveness. War was thousands of times greater in scale; its roots ran wide and deep all through the social soil; it affected everyone, and in the same ways as duelling affected its limited circle, though more severely. We might dissect the institution of war, sorting out for war, as we can for the institution of the duel, the sentiments of honour, the inertia of custom, the interests of social classes or the aims of statesmen. If we did this we should find parallels, but we should see more clearly how it was that war seemed not to be an institution capable of being brought under control, a subordinate institution within organized society, but a standing element of all social life. We should also see that the predominance of ethical opinion was against all duelling, but only against war when it was unjust; that duelling appeared radically unlike war because as an institution it could not be reconciled with the high purposes of organized society.

CHAPTER III

WAR AS A COLLISION OF SOCIETIES

IN 1932 two Russian historians, exiles in Germany, jointly published a book in which they gave an account of the history of the world from about the time of Mahomet to the war of 1914 according to those ideas which are known all over the world from the classical if cloudy argument of the Second Epilogue to Tolstoy's *War and Peace*.[1] Divesting themselves of many conceptions, and particularly of all belief in the influence of great men or of ideas on policies, they considered what might be called the visible aspect of the history of human masses, and called their book, in German, 'Military and Migratory Expeditions: World-history as Folk-movement'.[2] Whenever a large number of men are on the move, for whatever reason, and whether they are organized as an army or not, they may drive other armies or hordes or tribes or mobs of refugees away before them. They may also leave vacant spaces and even empty buildings and untended fields behind them into which other armed or unarmed migrants may follow. One moving mass thus moves another, either by pushing or by pulling, and economists explain this process in terms of optimum, excessive and deficient population. With much learning, ingenuity and consistency the brothers Kulischer trace connexions between all or almost all the recorded movements of popula-

[1] For a discussion of these ideas and of their place in the history of thought, see I. Berlin, *The Hedgehog and the Fox* (1953).

[2] A. and E. Kulischer, *Kriegs- und Wanderzüge: Weltgeschichte als Völker-bewegung*.

tions, whether by voluntary emigration, compulsory removals or military marches, together with fluctuations of the density of population in times of famine or epidemic.

The part of this book which concerns our period is not merely stimulating, but positively instructive. When the period began, the Chinese were expanding into Korea and all over south-east Asia. This went on in the late Ming period, from the later sixteenth century to 1644. After this there followed the eastward advance of Mongolian nomads, ending in the Manchu conquest of China, and the other nomad movement in the rear which supported the Moguls in India. Then there were the advance of the Russians against the Tartars, the settlement of the Dnieper under Polish nobles after the union of Lublin, the Swedish conquests at the expense of Russia, the German colonization to the east and the colonization of depopulated Brandenburg after the Thirty Years War by Dutch and German immigrants. In the wake of these came the expansion, first military and then civilian, of France, which had some of the most densely populated areas in Europe, ending with the dispersion of the Huguenots. The Habsburg conquest of Hungary followed. All of these were movements from west to east. At last, we are told, the world movement changed direction, and a new movement (of pushing, not pulling, structure) came in great waves over the Baltic lands, impelled in its turn by the Mongols, who were set in motion this time by the gigantic growth of the population of China from the last quarter of the seventeenth century.

If we were to examine all the stages of these processes we should certainly amplify and modify. We should not be content to skip the whole history of Ireland between the

Normans and the Famine. I suspect that we should find much to correct in the dates of the sequences that are alleged. We should have to pay attention to the numbers of the populations concerned, and to the way in which close social organization, as contrasted with the freedom of empty spaces, acts as a brake and slows the immigrants down. Our criticism would inevitably bring in many other questions of social organization, first of all the question why we should ignore the elements of discipline, command and policy, and treat the movements of fleets and armies as movements of population. We should have to analyse the attempts of governments to attract immigrants or to repel them, to engage foreign mercenaries or to let their own subjects out for hire. We should not be satisfied with treating these movements as movements and nothing else, for that is an abstract treatment. In practice it is the opposite of what these authors, and Tolstoy before them, intended to make of it, concrete history, innocent of laws or generalizations, using as its subject-matter only the lives of actual people. It is a behaviourist interpretation of the movements of people in terms of one single economic factor, the factor of population. It uses the conclusions of economic science; but it ignores the elements of will, purpose and political organization.

The external or behaviourist approach has its uses for historians as it has for other social scientists, but it belongs to the preparation of the materials. There is little need to justify this principle of method to historians, few of whom lose sight of it for long. Economists also, being for the most part still under the influence of the tradition of the economic man, tend to think in terms of conscious motives. It is among the anthropologists and sociologists that this special kind of determinism is common; but among them it is not universal. One sociologist whose point of view is not historical and who came to social studies with the training of a biologist has repudiated it in this matter of war. He maintains that modern war cannot be understood merely in terms of instinct by a study of individual or collective psychology, but only as a 'custom by which the highly organized States of modern times try to attain some political end'.[1]

With this reservation in mind we may consider some familiar historical interpretations of these wars. There is a familiar classification of the wars of the seventeenth century according to their aims. This distinguishes three main types of purpose for which the States went to war. No doubt other subsidiary or contributory causes actuated them, especially personal resentments and caprices; but I do not feel any doubt that they may be neglected. When Henri Quatre was making his warlike preparations at the time of his assassination, he may very well have thought now and again that if he invaded the Spanish Netherlands he might overtake the fugitive traitor Condé and his desirable princess, but it does not matter to us whether he thought about the lady or not. The greater issues have been classified, throughout this century, as religious, political and economic. The best way to discuss the value of this classification is not to treat the antecedents of wars in isolation, but to have in mind the whole character and consequences of the wars. Religion was part of the data of politics; its institutions and

---

[1] A. M. (now Sir Alexander) Carr-Saunders, *The Population Problem* (1922), p. 305.

ideas and the men who served it had all to be taken into account; they united or divided and so they supplied the statesmen with ends, means, methods and problems. In the first half of the century, religion and politics were inextricably mixed, but the mixture was not haphazard. It accorded with Europe's social and political condition. No Catholic or Protestant or Orthodox State avowedly declared war as a crusade against the opposite beliefs; but in every peace treaty when territory passed from one confession to the other, and often in the terms of the surrender of towns, there were clauses to define the rights, if any, which were to be reserved by the losers in matters of residence, worship, property and civil rights. During a war everyone knew that these things were at stake. It seems possible to distinguish armies and fleets in which many men of all ranks consciously fought for them from other armies and fleets which were not much moved by this stimulus. The Huguenots in Languedoc, the Camisards in the Cevennes, the New Model Army, the Cameronians, gained their drive and their discipline from it. But hardly a man can have been sustained only by his religious ardour. Normally, as might be expected, the higher his rank the less simple was the outlook of the fighting man. The general had to be something of a diplomatist; he had relations with his own government, with the civilian authorities of occupied territory, sometimes with the enemy commanders. He had to deal with supply, finance, administration, police. In their several degrees subordinate commanders too had to handle these things. The breadth of their education and of their sympathies probably corresponded more or less with the variety of their responsibilities. The statesmen were even further removed from the soldiery in the same direction. From an early stage of the Thirty Years War some observers thought that religion served them most often only as a pretext,[1] but even the least religiously minded statesman had to take account of confessional divisions as facts. An alliance with co-religionists was a simpler and more straightforward affair than a cross-division: Richelieu's relations with the Dutch and the Swedes or William III's relations with the imperial and Spanish ambassadors are the most obvious of many instances.

The religious element in wars weighed less in the seventeenth century than in the sixteenth, and less in the latter part of the seventeenth than in the earlier. All over Europe religion itself settled down into a less combative temper. The treaty settlements relating to it remained for the most part stable. Almost every region of Europe had been visited by religious wars, and almost the whole of it might now be mapped into areas of religious uniformity and areas of toleration. That was to a great extent the outcome of fighting. The States had become strong enough to disentangle politics from religion. Churches ceased to deflect the secular purposes of States in their relations with other States. These secular purposes, however, had this much of religion left in them that they were not ethically neutral. In the wars which were not called wars of religion, great principles were at stake. Englishmen and Dutchmen fought for the liberties of Europe, against Frenchmen who fought for their country and for their kings.

This is another way in which the religious element shades off into the political; and usually when we consider the political element, the element closest to the purposes of

[1] Crucé, *Nouveau Cynée*, p. 4.

57

States as such, it includes something of the others. Territorial aggrandizement may seem to be a purely political matter, but it brought with it control over the economic resources and the whole social and religious life of the territory. Sometimes, indeed, motives which must be classed as political seem to be present almost pure and unmixed, especially when liberty or liberties are at stake. There was the patriotic or nationalist motive to which I have referred. It appeared in different forms as circumstances moulded it: the French feeling was unlike the feeling which French invasions aroused in Germany, especially after the annexation of Strasbourg; the Portuguese feeling was different from the feeling of the Catalans, as their constitutional relations with Spain had been different. In some instances national feeling was mere feeling against the foreigner; in some it resulted from the deep incompatibility of two different orders of society. This was true of the resistance of Hugh O'Neill, earl of Tyrone, to the English. At the other extreme the issue was not merely who should rule, but what should be the constitutional forms of government. Bohemia in the Thirty Years War fought against a society much less alien in its social foundations than England was to Ulster, but one which wished to impose a definite structure of absolutism. The Dutch war of independence began in the same way in the sixteenth century; and in the seventeenth, this constitutional problem still had to be solved, along with the problem of the geographical extent of Spanish sovereignty, both in the northern and in the southern Netherlands. In Bohemia, in Ireland and in the Netherlands there were also religious antagonisms; these were three theatres of one great contest over religion which also embraced many other theatres. Its course and character depended on the local conditions, especially the political conditions, and, as was obviously necessary, the third element, the economic, crossed and combined with these at every point. Money provided the sinews of religious war as of any other, but wealth could be an end in itself; and scarcity, especially scarcity of food, was the most irresistible of enemies, and the most persuasive mediator of peace between exhausted adversaries.

The wars may be thought of as contests between armed forces or as contests between economic groupings; but the two sides in a war were never exactly the same from these two points of view and sometimes they were nowhere near coinciding. Every State recruited some of its soldiers and sailors from its own subjects. In former times the feudal obligation to military service had provided organized forces, and complementary rights of billeting and purveyance and so forth had given them the means of subsistence; but at the beginning of the century this system was obsolescent almost everywhere, and in some places, such as the Dutch republic, it was already obsolete. A newer method of raising troops was the exercise of sovereign rights over the whole population. In Sweden these two sorts of compulsion, merging into one another, were enough to set out a first-class field army, and in the latter part of the century a number of other States depended on conscription for some of their troops. Such troops, however, cost money; the decline of feudal military service was one aspect of the extension of money economy, and if troops had to be paid it was sometimes more desirable to hire foreign soldiers than to take men away from agriculture or industry at home.

Foreign troops could be acquired in many different ways.

Some enlisted as individuals in the existing formations. At sea crews were often very mixed,[1] but it was easier for the seafaring man to join a foreign ship than for a single recruit to find his way to a foreign army, especially if a different language was spoken in it. Some of the poorer countries had long been in business as bulk exporters of soldiers, either with or without some degree of state control on their movements. Throughout the century the Dutch States-General maintained English, Scottish and French regiments; the armies of the Thirty Years War were cosmopolitan; Louis XIV had English, Scottish, Irish, German, Spanish and Swiss units. Larger in scale than the recruiting of mercenaries, and in some ways simpler to organize, was the hiring of auxiliary troops in ready-made formations from their own governments. According to international law this letting-out of parts of its army or fleet did not involve a State in the war.[2] Such a State did indeed retain some degree of control, exactly what degree being a matter for agreement on each occasion. Not only minor German princes but the electors of Brandenburg and the kings of Denmark let out units of their armies, still holding them to their allegiance by oath. If they wanted to retain a high degree of control over the use of their troops, they entered a war as allies, that is, they committed themselves and their territories fully to its risks and claimed a voice in the policy it served, and a share in the gains.

---

[1] In the navy of Peter the Great all officers had to speak Russian, English and Dutch: *History of the Russian Fleet by a Contemporary Englishman* (1724), ed. Sir Cyprian Bridge (Navy Records Soc. 1899). This book gives valuable particulars of the conditions of service.

[2] Louis XIV did not recognize this principle, and made it a *casus belli* against Württemberg that it sent auxiliaries to the emperor in 1688.

Even if we disregard alliances it will be clear that the map of the sources of man-power in a war did not normally coincide at all closely with a map of the political components of the two sides; but if we turn from man-power to supply, we find a much greater divergence. Some States owned and managed their own establishments for making some of their supplies: for instance, there was a state monopoly of the manufacture of gunpowder in the Spanish Netherlands. But even State monopolies had to employ subcontractors, and for almost all their requirements of arms, ammunition, clothing, food, tents and transport the State had to buy from industry. The instances of miners or craftsmen working involuntarily under orders from the State are very few. This buying, like the hiring of troops, could be done abroad as well as at home. The exporting of arms was a branch of export industry which claimed government support like any other, at least when a State was at peace. Exporters, when left to themselves, deal freely with 'potential enemies'. Charles Davenant, the official statistician of the board of trade, could offer no explanation of the heavy French buying of English lead in 1662–3 unless it was for the French king's buildings or for a store of bullets.[1] It was again at the same level in 1699–1701 when there was no longer any question of roofing palaces, but the War of the Spanish Succession was impending.

The art of war had reached such a development that none of the States could supply itself within its own borders. The battle fleets of the English, French and Dutch could not exist without the timber and naval stores of Norway and the

---

[1] 'Report to the Commissioners of Public Accounts' (1711) in *Works*, v, (1771), 354; and Sir C. Whitworth, *State of the Trade of Great Britain* (1776).

Baltic. All Europe could not produce enough saltpetre for the gunpowder it consumed. Early in the century the emperors could not prevent the export of it from their hereditary dominions, whence some of it was carried by devious ways to the Turks.[1] The East India Company of London began to tap the Indian resources about the beginning of the reign of Charles I. By the middle of the century the Dutch were taking away far more saltpetre from India than the English. They also seem to have bought it from Englishmen both indirectly and directly for their war against the Commonwealth. The new charter of the company in William III's time obliged it to supply fixed quantities at fixed prices, and thus involved it in many difficulties. In war-time the shipments were insufficient; in peace-time they were unsaleable. It was impossible to organize an adequate national supply and at the same time to ensure that none of it could spill over abroad.[2]

Belligerents could buy from allies or neutrals or enemies, and there was never much difficulty in finding sellers who did not distinguish between solvent customers on these political lines. Most of the States tried with considerable success to prevent their own subjects from trading with their enemies; but none of them succeeded in this completely. The Dutch had financed their own war of independence by sea- and river-trade with their Spanish enemies, and throughout the century when they were in alliance with the English they never whole-heartedly co-operated in the

[1] E. Heischmann, *Die Anfänge des Stehenden Heeres in Österreich* (1925), p. 40.
[2] See the various references to saltpetre in B. Krishna, *Commercial Relations between India and England, 1601 to 1757* (1924), and S. A. Khan, *The East India Trade in the Seventeenth Century* (1923).

British policy of trying to stop all the trade of their own people with the French, a policy which at times the English would have liked to extend to a complete stoppage of all neutral trade with France. In every maritime war there were blockades and attempts to prevent trading in contraband, and their success depended on the action of fleets and on perpetually fluctuating agreements and disagreements with the neutrals. In the intervals between the wars the States tried to dictate the course of trade, often with an eye to future wars, by tariffs and boycotts. On the whole the commercial map of the European wars had been brought into closer conformity with the political map by the end of the period, but there were still great discrepancies. One of the clearest instances comes from the wars between Sweden and Denmark; in these, it has been truly written, 'Dutch capital, like Dutch shipping, fought on both sides'.[1]

These questions of recruiting and supply appear more intelligible if we disregard commodities and think in terms of money, but all the systems of public finance were complicated and no two of them were exactly alike. There does not seem to be any war for which figures are easily available, even for the great powers, showing what proportion of the war expenditure of each State, or of its total expenditure, was devoted to purchases abroad, or to the maintenance of foreign troops in the field. It is not easy to distinguish sums voted from sums annually spent, or to reconcile sums paid with sums received at the other end. Only a vague picture can be drawn even for the War of the Spanish Succession,

[1] Violet Barbour, *Capitalism in Amsterdam in the Seventeenth Century* (1950), p. III.

for which our information is better and easier to handle than for any of the others.[1]

How much a State could buy through the tortuous and interrupted channels of trade depended on the strength and adaptability of its finances. It depended, to begin with, on its success in getting a share of the wealth of the community, that is, on taxation and borrowing, and secondly on spending it economically and efficiently. The English, the French and the Dutch, and even less businesslike States such as Austria, were far more successful in these matters at the end of the period that at the beginning. From the time of the Protectorate to the time of William III the English reformed their taxation, banking and national debt, and their parliamentary system made a bridge between public and private finance. The French Crown proceeded in an entirely different way, but it used its centralized administrative system to emancipate itself from the control of foreign and private lenders. In 1690 an English diplomatist wrote: 'La France est si absolue que, tant qu'il y aura de l'argent, elle en trouvera.'[2] Their financial reforms, to which the needs of warfare were the main inducement, gave the States in the late seventeenth century a firmer hold on the wealth of their subjects than they had ever had before.

This was the more significant because on one side the financial reforms were part of a great economic movement, commonly called the rise of capitalism, by which the wealth

[1] The difficulties of these calculations may be seen by checking some of the figures in M. Braubach, *Die Bedeutung der Subsidien für die Politik im spanischen Erbfolgekriege* (1923) against C. T. Atkinson, 'The Cost of Queen Anne's War' in *Journal of Army Historical Research* (1955), pp. 174 ff.

[2] (W. Aglionby), *Quelques considérations sur la nécessité d'interdire le commerce des lettres avec la France* (1690).

of Europe was multiplied and reorganized. The new public finance had at its disposal not only greater taxable capacity but also a machinery of private finance which was able to carry out large international dealings. This made it possible for the wealth and ability of one country to operate in another, though not always as freely as if there had been no frontiers between the States. A foreign financier or entrepreneur sometimes found that definite laws or almost equally definite considerations of interest compelled him to become naturalized. In Denmark, Dutch bankers accepted landed estates in settlement of debts due to them by the Crown, but then the Danish king demanded an oath of allegiance from all landowners.[1] The mines and manufactures of Sweden were developed almost entirely by foreign, especially Dutch, capital and management; but a law was made in 1617 and enforced from time to time until well on in the eighteenth century which forbade merchants who had not been naturalized to remain in the country for more than two months in any year.[2] In spite of such impediments as these, financiers were able to operate for their own purposes or those of governments in every part of Europe. When they lent money they took security often in the form of industrial concessions, and they often stipulated for repayment in goods, or lent in order that goods of specified kinds might be bought from them or their associates. Thus finance helped forward commerce and industry, especially in war materials, and the economic history of the wars turned less on buying by governments from private traders than on the subsidies paid by one government to another or

[1] Barbour, *op. cit.* p. 117.
[2] See Appendix, no. 1 (at p. 101).

on loans from governments, and from private firms of lenders.

The outline of this international borrowing and lending is much clearer than that of the buying and selling. Throughout the century the Dutch were the great lenders, and among them the distinction between private lending and state lending was less important than anywhere else because the governing bodies of the republic paid more attention to business interests than those of any other State.[1] At the beginning, indeed, the republic had a war debt to the British Crown still outstanding, but this was settled in 1616. In that year money from the receipts of the Amsterdam admiralty was lent through an intermediary to the Elector of Brandenburg for his peaceful purposes; Gustavus Adolphus of Sweden, who began his war against Poland in the next year, borrowed from other Amsterdammers, and in 1619 the States-General paid a monthly subsidy to the ill-fated Frederick of the Palatinate. The Scandinavian kingdoms, the emperor, and a number of German cities and princes all depended on Holland at one time or another for their capacity to make war. Peter the Great of Russia failed to obtain loans, but he found other kinds of financial support there.

England also came into the Dutch sphere of financial influence. King Charles I had very little success in raising money there for the Civil War; Charles II failed to raise a loan, but Dutch capital sustained the Bank of England in some of its early difficulties, and thus Dutch financial support

[1] There is a convenient summary of the Dutch loans abroad in E. Baasch, *Holländische Wirtschaftsgeschichte* (1927), pp. 194 ff.; the loan of £2m. to Spain in 1667 mentioned on p. 206 appears to have been discussed but not actually paid.

in war-time took a special form to match the new British public finance. British governments no longer needed to ask for foreign loans. London was becoming a great money-market; it was ceasing to depend on Amsterdam and be-ginning to rival it as a centre of war finance. During the War of the Spanish Succession London began to lend abroad; in 1706 the first foreign loan was floated there, a quarter of a million for the emperor's army in Italy, to be paid on the order of Prince Eugene.[1] By this kind of business, and the official subsidies to continental allies, British capital entered on a new line of its own: it lent at home and abroad money which it borrowed abroad as well as at home. The sums involved were not yet very great, but the Bank of England, and the other great companies which financed the armies of Marlborough, attracted foreign, and naturally most of all Dutch, investors. The great alliances against France had thus an economic foundation in private as well as in state finance, and this meant that agriculture, industry and trade contri-buted to the war effort, if sometimes reluctantly, at an immense number of points. On the French side the internal economic structure was different. Authority played a greater part; and though its methods were less well-adapted to bring wealth to bear where it was needed, France had great resources at her disposal. French subsidies kept Gustavus Adolphus of Sweden in the field and Charles II of England out of it.

From the economic point of view the war may well seem less of a mêlée and more coherent, and writers on economic history have sometimes pressed this argument, at least for the latter part of the century, to an extreme conclusion.

[1] *Calendar of Treasury Books*, XXI, pt. 1 (1952), 109–10.

Werner Sombart repeated verbatim, without any modification and without full acknowledgement, the conclusion of Gustav von Schmoller that the Nine Years War and the War of the Spanish Succession were 'primarily the struggle of England and Holland against the growing industrial and commercial predominance of France, and against the dangers of the union of French trade with the commercial power of Spain'.[1] Schmoller's words come from an essay on mercantilism, the concept under which historians have grouped a variety of tendencies of economic thought and policy in a long period in which the seventeenth century is central. The concept is not so fashionable as it once was, but it is still often believed that there was a mercantilist era, prone to war, in which only exceptionally enlightened thinkers appreciated the economic advantages of pacific international trade.[2] Mercantilism is supposed to have promoted national wealth by many kinds of regulation, of rationalization and of encouragement, and then to have used all the resources of the State in peace and war to promote trade and population at the expense of other national communities. Starting from the principles that in commerce *nul ne gagne qu' autre ne perd*, that trade does not pay unless it yields a favourable money balance, that colonial trade and foreign trade bring in wealth which home trade only passes from hand to hand, mercantilism is alleged to be the *rationale* or the incitement for commercial and colonial wars. 'These wars', we are told, 'may be considered as struggles for the precious metals', and

---

[1] Schmoller, *The Mercantile System* (1884), pp. 66–7; Sombart, *Moderne Kapitalismus*, pt. 1 (1916) 440–1.

[2] This is a point of view from which the opinions of the leading economic writers are discussed in E. Silberner, *La guerre dans la pensée économique du XVIe et XVIIIe siècle* (1939).

'mercantilism as a money system was therefore largely responsible for this result; such was its most important direct political effect'.[1]

This way of thinking is replete with fallacies. Even when it does not assume that economic thought acts on policy and practice as an independent force from outside, it forgets that colonization and overseas trade had to be carried on with support from the States if they were to be carried on at all, and that, instead of arriving comfortably in empty spaces and welcoming markets, the European adventurers had to elbow their way where there was not room for all. It suggests that the statesmen worked in harmony with the business men in all kinds of international economic rivalry, and it ignores the recalcitrance of the many traders who tried to evade official protection. We may perhaps allow for all this, and retain the idea of mercantilism as a summary of the programmes of some persons in some places rather than as a system of principles underlying the facts of a whole era; but how much can we then accept of what we are told about its influence in the causation of wars? We must remember that it is a distortion to represent the mercantilist ideas as purely economic; they are concerned as much with political power as with wealth. They prevailed for the most part in monarchical countries where governments were extending their control over economic life and trying to bind the community closely together by harnessing every kind of power to their purposes. Although the Dutch republic also engaged in the competition for power it had different methods and different ideas; it allowed its citizens to trade wherever and however they could, and they in return supported it, with

[1] E. Heckscher, *Mercantilism*, II (1935), 182.

the profit motive for their incentive. But in neither kind of State could one system be exclusively followed. When Bacon wrote that King Henry VII preferred maxims of plenty to maxims of power, he drew a false antithesis. Economic warfare was waged in the interests of the States, but guns were fired in the interests of the traders.

In the second half of the century, when many causes had combined to intensify the protectionism of the greater States, the wars had economic preludes. In 1664, 1687 and 1702, for instance, the French were engaged in tariff wars before they began to fight; and when the real hostilities began, naval power was used with progressive effect to exert economic pressure. It is true that commercial pugnacity often prepared the way for armed conflict and led up to it by insensible degrees. Armed forces were used to seize land and factories (in both senses), ships and colonies, or to extort concessions in tariffs and navigation laws. But war and preparations for war also interrupted and frustrated the economic efforts of both the States and the traders. Some economic historians hold, in contrast with Schmoller and Sombart, that the Anglo-Dutch wars were mainly due to economic rivalry, but that in the struggle of the English and Dutch against Louis XIV economic considerations were overruled by political.[1]

Anyone who studies the details of trade war and war trade must be tempted to resign himself to the sceptical judgement of one eminent English economic historian that 'Policy in the sense of a deliberate, consistent and far-sighted scheme . . . is more often an illusion of the scholarly mind than a fact of history. Policy, as actually found in history, is a set of

[1] See, for instance, J. J. Reesse, *De suikerhandel van Amsterdam*, 1 (1908), 44.

devices into which a Government drifts under the pressure of practical problems and which gradually acquire the conscious uniformity of a type and begin, at last, to defend themselves as such'.[1] While admitting that there is a degree of truth in this, we can nevertheless define the channels through which the economic element operated in the wars. First of all, in spite of the disagreement of some distinguished historians, it seems to me well established that the demand for supplies and finance in war helped to promote the rise of large-scale capitalistic organization, and consequently the power of the great capitalists. Economic power can easily be converted into other kinds of power, and capitalism in turn called the States to its support. This is familiar from well-explored instances: we know how the Commonwealth government took up the long-standing quarrels of the English merchants against the Dutch, and how the court circle of Charles II threw itself into the enterprises of the 'imperialists' of the time. But there was always a tussle between the interests of trade as the traders understood them and the desire of the statesmen to control and direct economic affairs. Superficially the Hudson's Bay Company looks like an organ of aggression: its first three governors were Prince Rupert, James Duke of York, afterwards King James II, and John Churchill, afterwards Duke of Marlborough. But its accounts and minute-books have much to do with unimaginative business-men whose attention was concentrated on the prices of furs and the competition from interlopers.[2]

[1] G. Unwin, *Studies in Economic History* (1927), p. 184. The lecture there reprinted was delivered in 1913.

[2] See my two Introductions to the company's published minutes referred to under no. 9 in the Appendix, p. 152 below.

Whenever it came to a sharp opposition between them, however, economic considerations gave way before political considerations, especially considerations of the balance of power between States. Returning to the example of Anglo-Dutch relations in the first half of the century, we see that commercial rivalries all over the world repeatedly seemed to be leading to an outbreak of fighting in Europe when the graver prospect of political conflict sufficed to make the merchants on both sides suspend their mutual provocations. When the two States faced a common danger from outside, but only then, the two East India companies made mutual concessions. It was so when Henry IV of France was assassinated, when the Dutch were weakened by their revolution of 1618, and when the British broke with Spain in 1625. Between the crises the diplomatists on both sides, with better information and more foresight than the merchants, used their influence to compose the merchants' quarrels, but with little success. Even in the second half of the century, when the statesmen espoused the policy of economic aggression, it was still, though less visibly, apt to be overruled. Both English and Dutch merchants had to abandon a good many claims and ambitions when the two States became allies against Louis XIV. Adam Smith was justifying the practice of the seventeenth century against some of the economic doctrines of his own age when he wrote, in connexion with the Act of Navigation, that defence is of much more importance than opulence.

In considering the economic aspect of the wars we have noticed several times the contrast between the two halves of our period. In particular, we have seen that in the second half war was waged on a far larger scale and the States exercised a firmer control over their peoples and their material resources. These changes in combination with many others constitute the great historical occurrence to which Professor Roberts has given the name of the Military Revolution.[1] Professor Roberts took as his starting-point the art of war on land, that is, the armament, training and tactical use of infantry, cavalry, artillery and engineers. He showed that the consequences of the new methods of the great commanders from Maurice of Nassau to Charles XII were not merely military, but affected the administrative systems, the constitutions and the economy of the States. He pointed to the complementary effects of the related changes in sea warfare. He concluded that by 1660, with mass armies, strict discipline, the new military hierarchy, applied science and ruthlessness, among other things, a great and permanent change came over the European world. I am glad to have this opportunity of saying that I have found on every page of his compact exposition something new and valuable. Not the least valuable point is the title, the phrase which sums up the whole.

This revolution was as complex as the societies which it transformed; but when it is understood the complexities do not look like mere confusion. With the help of Professor Roberts's chronological searchlight we can at last begin to see the fighting, not as a *mêlée*, but as a process in which order, first of some kinds, then of others, comes into view, perhaps to remain, perhaps to recede again into darkness. At the beginning of the period the wars were not continuations of religious or dynastic or economic or any other policy by the use of organized force, but collisions of com-

[1] M. Roberts, *The Military Revolution, 1560–1660 (s.a.*, published in 1956).

munities. Some of these communities were the imperfect and improvised assemblages of civil war, others were the comparatively complete societies called monarchies or republics. They sometimes blundered into their struggles and sometimes went into them methodically, with their eyes open, through the regular procedure of negotiation, ultimatum and declaration of war; sometimes they managed hostilities equally methodically, but sometimes their forces, even if they did not become mutinous or barbarous, were not servants at all but were moved by a will of their own. Peace sometimes came by rational stages, but sometimes by exhaustion and anarchy. Any component part of society might break loose and smash or obstruct any other in its movements.

Even at the end of the period there was still something of all this, for war is destruction; but one side of the military revolution was a great strengthening of the control of the States over war. We have already considered the parallel change, which in fact is another part of a more comprehensive change which includes them both, in the minor institution of the duel. We have seen that it came, not through a bare assertion of sovereign will, but through thought and contrivance and as a resultant of many social forces pressing in different directions. We are thus prepared to find that every element of society was involved in the *étatisation* of war. At sea there was at first no clear line between war and peace. In peace-time an armed ship might be a merchantman, but she might carry a commission authorizing her to capture vessels of another flag in reprisal for some act of robbery, or she might be a plain pirate. In war-time the States requisitioned some of the merchant-ships for fighting or transport and commissioned others as privateers; but warships and privateers alike were apt to engage in smuggling, in trading with the enemy, in accepting ransom for their prizes instead of carrying them into port, and even in worse malpractices. By the end of the period the seas were policed; maritime law was better defined and better enforced; when there was war there were no privately owned ships in the line of battle, and in peace-time yachtsmen cruised in the Narrow Seas for pleasure. On land the armies no longer contained feudal levies or mercenaries hired from contractors; they were recruited, paid, equipped and managed by the States. *Le roi seul a droit de glaive*[1] was a known principle, and it won recognition through the military revolution. In England there was a turning-point when General Monck put an end to the interventions of the army in politics. He told his officers that 'nothing was more injurious to discipline than their meeting in council to discuss civil things'. He had been trained in the Dutch service, where, as he truly said, 'soldiers received and observed commands, but gave none'.[2] One by one the armies of Europe, including the generals, conformed to this rule and even improved upon it. In the British army, for instance, there was a further stage when Queen Anne's government took notice of the prevailing practice of buying and selling commissions, and regulated it. The State was extending its control to the social groundwork of its armed forces. For once I will venture beyond the limits of this period, hazarding the generalization that from 1660 until 1779 the States of Europe were nearer to a monopoly of force than they had ever been before. They were struggling into a position *au dessus de la mêlée*.

[1] See above, p. 29.
[2] C. H. (afterwards Sir Charles) Firth, *Cromwell's Army* (1902), pp. 383–5.

CHAPTER IV

WAR AND THE EUROPEAN COMMUNITY

IN my second lecture I referred to the romantic mis-representation of the duel as an elegant, if dangerous, incident in civilized social relations. There is a similar view of war which is held by so many historians that it must be examined. Professor Arnold Toynbee, in a section of his *Study of History* on 'The impact of democracy and industrialism on War', expresses it in a statement which, if we accept it, must be of high importance for modern history generally, and in particular for the history of war, of political democracy and of religion. 'The fundamental reason why, in our world, War was less atrocious in the eighteenth century than it has been in the nineteenth and twentieth centuries is that, in the eighteenth century, when war was no longer being used as an instrument of ecclesiastical policy and had not yet begun to be used as an instrument of national policy, there was an interval during which War was merely the sport of kings.' This idea is expressed in varying formulations in other parts of the same section, and also in an appendix dealing with 'Militarism and the military virtues'. Here is one of the variants: 'This age of relatively "civilized" warfare...began when the institution of war was disconnected from the driving force of sectarian Religious Fanaticism at the close of the seventeenth century.' The point of time is stated more precisely here, and there is a change from ceasing to use war as an instrument of ecclesiastical policy to disconnecting it from the driving force of religious fanaticism.[1] Another facet of the idea is revealed in a third passage which refers to a date in the third quarter of the seventeenth century, so that we need not take the words 'eighteenth century' and 'close of the seventeenth century' in the first two passages to be meant precisely. The third passage follows after a sprightly comparison between the consideration which the eighteenth-century soldiers 'usually displayed to the civilian population' and the hunting man's sportsman-like considerateness for the farmers' gate and fences: 'The attitude of eighteenth-century war-makers on this point comes to light in the almost unanimous and unmistakably genuine indignation to which they were moved by a few flagrant breaches of the rule: for example by the devastation of the Palatinate by Louis XIV in A.D. 1674 and 1689 and the devastation of the Neumark and Cüstrin by the Russian army in 1758.'[2]

To discuss Dr Toynbee's view of eighteenth-century warfare would be to transgress the limit which I have set for these lectures,[3] but it is within my subject to inquire how far he is right in contrasting the latter part of our period with the earlier. The last passage which I quoted speaks of 'the almost unanimous and unmistakably genuine indignation' to which war-makers themselves were moved by a few flagrant breaches of 'the rule' against mishandling civilians. The words 'almost unanimous' appear too em-

---

[1] See p. 56 above.

[2] These passages will be found in vol. IV, 143, 147, and vol. VI, 640 (1939 ed.).

[3] I do not, however, accept it. What appears to me the true view, that the tempering of eighteenth-century warfare by courtesy was a 'vernis d'emprunt' is admirably stated by A. Sorel, *L'Europe et la révolution française*, I (1885), 81–8.

phatic. Louis XIV can scarcely be blamed for the devastation of the Palatinate in 1674. His general, Turenne, seems to
have intended it to make the country impossible for his
opponents, but he disclaimed responsibility. He tried to
placate his indignant kinsman, the elector Palatine, who at
first challenged him to a duel and taunted him with having
become cruel after his conversion to Rome.[1] There were
French soldiers and French civilians in high office who
expressed misgivings about the wisdom of the second devastation of the Palatinate and were shocked by its brutality.
It was the most thorough application within the limits of
the historical consciousness of western Europe of what we
now call a 'scorched-earth' policy. Other such things had
occurred not very long before in the Baltic region and, on
a smaller scale, further west. The sufferers now were the
inhabitants of every rank from the prince-bishop of Mainz
to the burghers and the peasants, and one of them, sym-
pathizing with the people among whom she was born, was
the sister-in-law of King Louis XIV himself, Louise Charlotte
of the Palatinate. But the devastation was not a wholly
unsuccessful operation of war; it did not dislodge Louvois,
the minister who planned it, and the protests against it came
mainly from the countries which were opposed to Louis in
the war. Marlborough took similar action, although on a
smaller scale, in the next war when he laid waste part of
Bavaria after Blenheim. He never did it except on this
occasion; but honesty compels us to admit that he never
fought any other campaign on soil which he could have
laid waste to his own military advantage. The indignation

[1] A. M. de Ramsay, *Vie de Turenne* (ed. of 1771), II, 254ff.; C. G. Picavet,
Les dernières années de Turenne (s.a., ? 1919), pp. 408–10.

aroused by the devastation of Louvois does not imply a new and more humane phase of opinion.[1]

Throughout the seventeenth century, although the institution of war was accepted as at worst a necessary evil, there were protests against cruelty to civilians as well as soldiers. Some of those which belong to the period of the Thirty Years War are so eloquent that they have never been forgotten. In German literature the devastations, especially of the Swedes in the later years, provided matter for the savage satire of Grimmelshausen's *Simplicissimus*. Jacques Callot, a native of Franche-Comté, in his two, still familiar, series of etchings published in 1632–3, represented all the miseries of war, and especially the burning of homes, the looting, the murders and the ravishings.[2] Perhaps in these the note of protest is deflected by a taste for the macabre; but at any rate in his choice of subjects Callot was carrying on an old-established tradition, and it went on in the next generation. Romeyn de Hooghe, the most talented Dutch engraver of his time, made famous all over Europe the names of Bodegrave and Swammerdam, two Dutch villages which were burnt in the winter of 1672–3 with accompaniments of horrible cruelty. If, in this matter, there seems to be a contrast between the earlier part of the century and the later it is not because a few flagrant outrages aroused a new kind of indignation. It was a reflexion of the change in the scale and the systematizing of war. In cruelty, as in many other things, Louvois 'n'a rien inventé: il n'a fait que régulariser, en quelque sorte, les usages établis, et appliquer avec

[1] K. von Raumer's *Die Zerstörung von der Pfalz* (1930) is valuable for the facts, but its emotional tone has other origins.

[2] See E. A. Beller, *Propaganda in Germany during the Thirty Years War* (1940), for other instances.

méthode les procédés que ses contemporains employaient avec confusion'.[1] There is no reason to suppose that the protests came from some new state of mind among the victims or those who sympathized with them, among the war-makers or outside their number: they represent the reaction of the old human nature to these new overt facts.

So far as they were publicly expressed in anything more than incidental phrases or purposeless laments, they were expressed by writers on the opposite side to the perpetrators. The French objected loudly when the English threw explosive shells into their seaport towns, but they themselves had used them not only against Algiers in 1683, when the bomb-ketch was a new invention, and again in 1688, but also against Genoa in 1684. Queen Mary of England was moved by the ruin of the poor and innocent inhabitants of the French towns, and she was indignant, but against the French who had begun such practices 'even in full peace' and forced others to retaliate.[2] Here, however, I would underline the words of Dr Toynbee that the protests were 'unmistakably genuine'. If genuineness can be tested by looking at the protests themselves, we may certify it even in many of the pamphlets and pictures about atrocities that were made by paid propagandists. It must, indeed, be admitted that sometimes a sincere protest proved so effective that afterwards it was repeated when the original emotion behind it had worn away. In 1624 the news arrived in England that ten Englishmen had been executed after torture by the Dutch at Amboyna in the Moluccas on a charge of treason. In London it was believed that this was a judicial murder, done

[1] Sorel, *op. cit.* I, 83.
[2] G. Burnet, *Essay on the Memory of the Late Queen* (1695), pp. 171–2.

for reasons of policy. There was spontaneous rage, but the court of the East India Company, whose policy was to withstand the Dutch, exploited it by publishing narratives of the 'massacre', and they hired a painter to make a picture of the torture scene. The Privy Council checked them; but in later times, when Great Britain was at war with the Dutch, the government hired pamphleteers to revive this memory, and, as late as 1673, John Dryden took it as the subject of a play which seems to have nothing behind it except hatred, prejudice, or artificial anger. No one can tell in what proportions true and feigned feelings were mixed in men's minds; but we can be sure that there was, as there had been for ages before, genuine and disinterested indignation. Critics who trace the continuities of literary and artistic forms would, indeed, be able to show that the pamphlets about Amboyna, with their woodcuts, carry on the tradition of the books of martyrs which had their beginnings in early times and provided both Catholic and Protestant Europe with popular reading from the Reformation all through the sixteenth and seventeenth centuries.

Two ideas which have been very popular among our contemporaries have been brought together and used to put an interpretation on these utterances, the historical idea that Puritanism was an outgrowth of the rising middle class and the psychological idea that repressed tendencies of our natures assert themselves in the form of moral indignation against those same tendencies when we detect them in others. Thus we are told that atrocity propaganda against enemies is an expression of puritan, that is, middle-class psychology. One author has been at pains to estimate the number of passages in the Thomasson collection of tracts where this sentiment occurs. On the foundation of more than 250 footnote references he erects the conclusion 'that the Puritans as a group, in contradistinction to the Cavaliers, were characterized by a strong disposition to indulge in a number of those kinds of sin which they indignantly denounce [*sic*] in others'.[1] This may be psychologically truer than the crude accusation of the Royalists that it was the way of the Puritans to 'compound for sins they are inclined to By damning those they have no mind to';[2] but there is no attempt to prove that in comparable circumstances the Puritans, or the armies of the Parliament and the Commonwealth, who were not all puritans by any means, did behave differently from their opponents. Nothing is said about what severities were permitted and what condemned by the laws and customs of war, and there is no comparison between the very unequal opportunities of the two sides to print propaganda which they thought likely to impress the ordinary, not puritan, man. Nor do I believe that a study of two sets of journalistic scribblers has anything like the value of a comparison between the leaders of thought who stood above them.

So much for protests and propaganda. But was there in fact a mitigation of the sufferings of civilians in war? Before the military revolution everyone took it for granted that peasants hated soldiers. They had good reason for it, and often enough they revenged the outrages that they suffered. There is no need to refer to Callot's pictures, or the Clubmen in Dorset, or the hostility of the Hungarian peasantry to the Christian armies in the Turkish wars. What difference did

[1] S. Ranulf, *Moral Indignation and Middle Class Psychology* (1938), pp. 77–94.
[2] S. Butler, *Hudibras* (1663), part 1, canto 1.

the military revolution make here? Adam Smith said in a lecture in 1763: 'It is the interest of the general not to rob the peasants, because it would be difficult to march an army carrying all its provisions through the country of an enemy. But by engaging them to stay he is supplied without any other expedient. By this means war is so far from being a disadvantage in a well-cultivated country, that many get rich by it. When the Netherlands is the seat of war all the peasants grow rich, for they pay no rent when the enemy is in the country and provisions sell at a high rate.'[1] Whether this was true at the time when it was said does not concern us now, but it looks like an optimistic interpretation of one specific seventeenth-century change. In 1625 Grotius referred to the Dutch War of Independence, during which he was born and grew up, as one in which agriculture was carried on safely in no man's land (*in collimitio*) on paying tribute to both parties, apparently implying that this was no longer the practice.[2] Later, in the course of the Thirty Years War, Gustavus Adolphus abandoned the practice of pillaging towns which were captured after refusing to capitulate, and others followed him. A general revival of the system of regular exactions of money from the countryside is implied by the words of Vattel: 'au pillage de la Campagne et des lieux sans défense, on a substitué un usage, en même temps plus humain, et plus avantageux au Souverain qui fait la guerre: c'est celui des Contributions.'[3] I do not know

---

[1] *Lectures on Justice, Police, Revenue and Arms* (ed. E. Cannan, 1896), p. 273. As he did not include this argument in the admirable statement of his views on armies in *The Wealth of Nations*, bk. v, c. 1 (1776), it is at least possible that Adam Smith ceased to be satisfied with it.

[2] *De jure belli ac pacis*, III, XII, iii, 2.

[3] *Le droit des gens*, II (1758), 136.

6-2

whether historians have traced the coming of this change through the records; but it does not seem to have brightened the lives of the peasantry in our period. In the winter of 1676–7 the Dutch pensionary Fagel told Sir William Temple that in Flanders the country was 'growing desolate by the unsettled contributions'.[1] A careful Belgian historian has reaffirmed the accepted opinion that the Nine Years War inflicted poverty and misery on the agricultural population in the Spanish Netherlands.[2] During the War of the Spanish Succession it may well be that many peasants fared better than those in the immediate neighbourhood of Ramillies or Oudenarde or Malplaquet; but there cannot be any doubt that the Anglo-Dutch condominium of 1706–13 pressed hard on the agricultural producers.

Besides the disinterested and interested protests there were practical restraints on the excesses of war and there were efforts to improve these restraints. In the armies themselves there was discipline, and it was well understood that up to a point good discipline in a fighting force was to the advantage not only of that force but also of those which were opposed to it. The articles of war promulgated by the different States had an international circulation among commanders. A German compiler[3] put together twelve of these codes in a book to which he gave the title *Corpus juris*

---

[1] Temple, *Memoirs*, 1672–9 (1692), p. 216.

[2] J. A. van Houtte in *Mededeelingen van de koninklijke vlaamache Akademie, Klasse der letteren*, Jaarg. xv (1953), no. 8, 20–21. See also L. van der Essen in *L'université de Louvain à travers cinq siècles* (1927), for clear explanations of the various kinds of requisitioning which impoverished the countryside. A matter which deserves investigation is the rationing of food supplies in these provinces during the war, for which there are materials, among other places, in the Heinsius papers in the Rijksarchief at the Hague.

[3] Petrus Pappus von Tratzberg; see above, p. 39, n. 1.

militaris (1665). He included a drill-book and prayers
suitable for use in the field, and in another edition (1674)
he added two new sets of articles, those of Brunswick-
Lüneburg and the imperial articles issued at Ratisbon in
1673.[1] In the sixteenth century there had already been
articles against killing draft animals and dairy-cows. In the
seventeenth they were extended to protect arable fields,
meadows and gardens; but the legitimacy of taking booty
from an enemy was not called in question.[2]

From time to time commanders in the field entered into
agreements with one another, as they had always done,
about such matters as the ransoming and exchanging of
prisoners of war. The history of such agreements is obscure,[3]
and I do not know whether it underwent important changes
in the seventeenth century; but towards the end of the
century they sometimes included rules of discipline which
were to be enforced by the courts martial of the two armies
concerned. There was such a clause in a cartel of 1692
between the French on the one hand and the representatives
of the emperor, two of the German circles and the Duke of
Württemberg on the other. It regulated the size and com-
position of military parties sent out to collect contributions
in a theatre of war. If any such party went out without an
officer or with fewer than nineteen unmounted or fifteen
mounted men, they were to be treated by both sides as
robbers and they were to be liable to two months' imprison-

---

[1] Montecuccoli, writing before these imperial articles appeared, recommended those of different countries for different purposes. *Opere*, ed. Grassi,
I, 83, 132; II, 145.

[2] F. Redlich, *De praeda militari: looting and booty, 1500–1815* (*Vierteljahrschrift
für Sozial- und Wirtschaftsgeschichte, Beiheft* 39, 1956). This writer gives titles of
some later editions of the Corpus.

[3] See Appendix, no. 11.

ment. No commander wanted his men to go off raiding the countryside without proper control. That led to outrages against the country-folk and to resentment, if not to retaliation, on their part. The good will of the population was always worth something and might be vitally important. Besides that, looting led to quarrels among the marauders themselves, to neglect of their duties, to absence without leave and to desertion. On the other hand, if the enemy's standards of discipline were lower than one's own, it was impossible to prevent unauthorized reprisals and retaliatory atrocities. In the late seventeenth century therefore each of the great belligerent States did something to bring its armed forces under better control. They followed one another's examples and studied one another's regulations, and they even made some agreements for this purpose with their opponents in war.

Whether these agreements were effective or not, it is certain that there was a great improvement in the discipline of European fleets and armies. The opportunity for this resulted from the improved administrative systems and especially from the improved finances. These enabled the States to pay their armies better and so to end the chronic danger of mutiny and desertion which haunted the ill-paid armies of the sixteenth century and the Thirty Years War. There were, however, some international agreements of another type which were also meant to mitigate the severity of war. The same cartel that I have quoted contained a number of clauses which seem to have been so intended. The most remarkable of these imposes the death penalty for the use, against either man or beast, of missiles of tin or any other metal than lead, of poisoned projectiles, or (?) wire or otherwise irregularly shaped missiles. I hope I am only admitting a deficiency in my own knowledge and not pointing out a field where research is needed, when I say that I have not discovered whether this clause appeared now for the first time, or who proposed it and why, and whether it found imitators or produced any result. Its signing was not an isolated incident. Two years earlier a writer of Strasbourg, a city then in French occupation though not yet ceded to France by the empire, had proposed that the bombardment of cities should be prohibited because of the losses of civilian lives, and that bombs, red-hot balls and other destructive missiles should be forbidden.[1] In 1698 another German writer argued in the same sense *De armis illicitis*. He condemned the weapons mentioned in the cartel and all others that were meant to do injuries which could serve no legitimate military purpose.[2]

These attempts to humanize the laws of war had no direct effects that we can trace. In becoming more regular it did, indeed, become in some ways more humane, and there were certain kinds of pressure which restrained both commanders and governments from contravening the laws of war as their opponents understood them. Sometimes a threat of reprisals had this effect, as when the French forced one of the generals of William III to cancel an order for sending Irish prisoners

[1] This book is summarized by J. G. Bluntschli in an article referred to by E. Nys in his *Droit international* (ed. of 1912), III, 147, but I have not succeeded any better than Nys in tracing a copy of it. The author was Justin Gentil.

[2] The author, Johann Georg von Birckholtz, is described as *miles Saxonicus*, The name is that of an important military and official family in the Polish-Saxon service, and I should identify the writer as Johann Georg von Birckholtz auf Liebstadt, Zuschendorff und Krebs: J. H. Zedler, *Universal Lexicon*, III, (1733) *s.a.* The little book was a doctoral dissertation in the law faculty at Heidelberg. The 'promotor' Heinrich Cocceius was in the service of the elector of Brandenburg and the book was published at Frankfurt-am-Oder.

to servitude in the West Indies.[1] Sometimes actual reprisals were used successfully, as when William III rearrested his prisoner, Marshal Boufflers, because, in breach of a cartel, the French had forced some soldiers of two captured garrisons to take service in their own army.[2] In the same war, when the British and the Dutch attempted to use their naval power against French commerce with a complete disregard of neutral rights, it was partly the opposition of the neutrals which frustrated the attempt. The proposals to limit the permissible weapons seem to have won no support from interests which could bring such pressure to bear.

Some writers conclude that nothing except lack of power restrained seventeenth-century commanders and statesmen from resorting to any and every means of damaging an enemy. In 1649–50 the Venetian inquisitors of state took a good deal of trouble to send off to Crete a certain Dr Michael Angelo, whose purpose was to infect the Turkish army with his 'quintessence of the pest'. The officer chiefly responsible in the matter did indeed justify this essay in biological warfare by the old crusading argument: 'in my opinion the usual considerations do not apply to the Turks, who are enemies by religion, treacherous by nature and who have betrayed your excellencies'.[3] The great Montecuccoli, however, did not qualify his eighth maxim for an invader in that way: 'to throw pestilential vapours against them; to destroy the surrounding countryside, the farmsteads, the mills; to

---

[1] R. Lee, *Treatise of Captures in War* (1759), p. 245.

[2] Macaulay, in his *History*, ed. Firth, v (1914), 2526, 2534–6, tells the story, but says that the two garrisons had been sent as prisoners to France. The point is correctly stated by O. Klopp, *Der Fall des Hauses Stuart*, vii (1879), 99.

[3] V. Lamarsky, *Secrets d'état de Venise* (1884), pp. 128–41; the passage translated is on p. 130.

rot them with contagious diseases; to sow dissensions among their people.'[1]

Their purposes may have been ambiguous and their consequences negligible; yet the official and unofficial writings against total war did amount to something. Their basis was humanitarian reasoning which could have been universally and impartially applied to friends and enemies alike. That they were written implies the existence of an audience whose approval they might gain, and, indeed, there was such an audience. There was a European community, itself a member of a nebulous and loosely knit world-wide community, within which the wars took place. It does not appear, however, that this community became more effective or more visible during the century in the sense that there either was, or was believed to be, any important movement towards the humanizing of war or towards limiting its political aims. These two things are not the same, though they have often been confused, and historians who find them both in the eighteenth century follow a succession of writers which begins, as far as I know, not earlier than Voltaire. Voltaire was nineteen years old at the time of the peace of Utrecht. He never, I believe, suggested that the wars of Louis XIV were more temperate or more humane than those of earlier ages. If there was a real movement in this direction it must have left traces in our historical authorities. There may very well be pamphlets, of greater or less importance, in which the world is exhorted to humanity or congratulated on achieving it—I do not know—but it will be more significant if we can find such expressions in the papers that circulated among men of action. There are instances of

[1] *Opere*, I, 153.

officers who had a bad reputation for cruelty, and of others who were taken to task for undue mildness. As in all other periods there is sometimes a contrast between the ferocious amateur soldier and the comparative mildness of the professional who likes things to be done properly; but we are not in a position to trace any general movement towards restraint.

It is perhaps worth while to spend a moment on clearing away one misunderstanding. Commanders in the field sometimes used flags of truce to exchange compliments or presents, and they exchanged messages in terms of ceremonious politeness. There are so many instances of their using these occasions to pick up useful oddments of information, or to insinuate invitations to treachery, that we should be very innocent if we attached any importance to this pleasing custom. It did not mean that war was not deadly earnest. A profound historical thinker has pointed out that in many different ages and environments war has shown, as the duel showed, the 'ludic' element of punctilious or even courteous correctness, the formality of a game.[1]

If we reject the idea that the European community was growing more effective through the limiting of war, we need not fall back on the view that international relations were a mere mêlée. There was another way in which the community became more coherent, and the clearer ordering of the relations between States, even in war, brought a degree of steadiness into the confusion. My third conclusion, indeed, is that the wars not only took place within that community but that, while in some respects they interfered with it, in others they made it more actual and furthered its

[1] J. Huizinga, *Homo ludens* (1940), reprinted in *Verzamelde Werken*, v (1950), 117–33.

purposes. Europe was a community then in the sense that men were associated in it, more closely or less closely, more willingly or less willingly, for a great number of social purposes. The idea is familiar when we think of Europe as a community bound together by economic relations, which were closer within it than between it and the rest of the world. It is even more familiar when we think of religion (in spite of the confessional divisions) or of letters and learning and the fine arts. In these departments the wars interrupted intercourse but they did not disrupt or destroy the community. During the Anglo-Dutch wars the English continued to learn from Dutch technology and business organization. During the wars of Louis XIV, French influences spread over England and Germany. William III brought French painters and the talented architect Daniel Marot to England, and as artists they were no less French for being Huguenot refugees. In 1673, when he was commanding the Dutch forces against the English, William III and his friend Bentinck bought locks and gloves and perfumed powder in London.[1] These trifles will serve as symbols of a state of mind. More to our purpose is the legal aspect of the community, the acceptance within it of rules and practices of international law in peace and, up to a point, in war, on land and sea. Less commonly noticed than any of these are some of the social foundations of the European community, which, if we examine them, will show that the destructive institution of war had a constructive international value.

Europe was coming to be divided into sovereign terri-

[1] *Correspondentie van Willem III en Bentinck*, ed. N. Japikse, 2nd ed., 1 (1932), 176.

torial States, and within its own boundaries each State presided over an articulated social order. At the head of this social order were the ruling dynasties, and the usual way of explaining international affairs was to enumerate the rights and pretensions of the princes. In later times it was, indeed, customary to contrast the dynastic wars of this period with the national wars of the age which began with the French Revolution. The new national ambitions, however, carried on many of the older pretensions, and, since these were claims which the dynasts made as heads of States, to say that war had a dynastic element is scarcely more than saying that it was an affair of the States of the period. The framework of Europe was mainly dynastic. There were, indeed, a few elective monarchies. Some of these became hereditary, and the persons elected as monarchs often belonged to dynasties which had a prescriptive right to be elected or were members of families who ruled by hereditary right elsewhere. There were also republics, but the Dutch Republic was the only one which took a leading part in the wars, and it was concerned in dynastic affairs both through the family connexions of its stadholders of the Nassau and Orange-Nassau families and also because it used its influence in the marriage and succession questions of other States. Weakness or geographical position made some of the republics pacific, but there is no reason to think that freedom from monarchy by itself had this effect.

The French general Feucquières drew no distinction between monarchies and republics in the matter of pugnacity: 'j'ai vu l'Europe continuellement agitée par l'ambition des Princes et des Républiques'.[1] The Dutch Republic was

---

[1] A. M. de Pas, marquis de Feucquières (Feucquière), *Mémoires* (ed. of 1737), I, 7, 28. This was written during the later years of Louis XIV.

exempt from one characteristic ambition, that for territorial gains: its interests were maritime, and its constant policy was to maintain its shipping and its possessions overseas without advancing its land frontiers. That, however, did not mean that it was more pacific than its neighbours. A well-informed Englishman wrote of it in 1614: 'Every Man seemeth to affect Warr, as the Meane to enlarge the generall and inrich every particular; Peace hurteth and weakeneth.'[1] Only under the stress of heavy losses in the wars against the English and Louis XIV did Dutch political writers maintain that the interest of a trading nation is peace. The period during which England was a republic was bellicose. Elsewhere I cannot recall any writer of much authority who believed that a government based on consent was less likely to resort to war than an absolute monarchy.

Except in the republics, sovereignty, with or without constitutional limitations, was a possession of a person. Those who held it were subject to all the influences which make the owner of any kind of property, or the holder of any office, apt to magnify it and desirous at least of handing it on undiminished to his successor. In this they were helped and hindered by the attractions and antipathies which kinship always implies, and their diplomacy worked in this *milieu*. Dynastic policy might be warlike but it was not held to be, and indeed it was not, necessarily so. Sometimes dynastic consideration counted against war. When Richelieu worked for war against the emperor Ferdinand II he had to overcome the opposition of the emperor's niece, who was Queen of France. It would be hard to say whether the Habsburg marriage-net did more to divide

[1] See p. 95 of part II, no. 10 in the Appendix, below p. 152.

Europe or to keep harmony between Spain and Austria and between the States which had reasons for being friendly with them. In the same way all the other unions and affiliations of the dynasties were worked into the peace settlements and the friendly relations of States as well as into their offensive alliances. This system had disadvantages of which everyone was aware. Far too much depended on the survival or the health of heirs and heiresses. But it did not in its nature cause the selfish interests of a few families to override the interests of their subjects. The greatness of the monarchs depended on keeping their subjects together in some sort of loyalty to them. They were symbolic heads as well as legal sovereigns. Their marriages were political contracts, and they more often subordinated their personal lives to their public functions than vice versa. James I increased his unpopularity in England by sacrificing his family tie with the elector palatine to the changed exigencies of his policy. The great Earl of Strafford wrote: 'nor do alliances and marriages rise to stand between Princes when their ambitions or safetys are cast into the balance'.[1] Dynastic motives were not so much a cause of wars as an element in international relations whether they were rough or smooth.

The kings and princes, with their special education and ceremonial attributes, formed, as we know, a circle. It was not a caste absolutely closed to newcomers: the Medici had risen into it recently; the House of Orange completed their ascent by the coronation of King William III; the German electors were half-way through the door, and, in fact, there was no hard and fast line between royalties and the highest

[1] I owe this extract from his letter to John Taylor (of 7 September 1633) (in the Fitzwilliam Papers, Central Library, Sheffield) to the kindness of Dr C. R. Fay.

nobility; but *Gottesgnadentum* was a reality, and the rulers could only keep their distance if they were very particular about marrying. Lauzun was imprisoned for aspiring to marry Mademoiselle. In the simple and sparsely populated Europe of those days an exclusive policy in royal marriage alliances meant that the dynasties had to be international, though no ruler in the century so much as thought of a marriage alliance outside Europe, and there were no marriages between Russian imperial princes or princesses and those of the West.

This international character of the dynasties was one of the bonds of the European community, such as it then was; it was one of the elements of international relations that when one king thought of another he thought of him as a brother-in-law or more or less a distant cousin.[1] But it mingled strangely with another element. With few exceptions the kings were soldiers, and, as Professor Roberts has pointed out, by the close of the century, when armies normally wore uniforms, 'there was already a tendency in monarchs of an absolutist cast to consider military uniform as their normal attire—as Charles XII did, for instance, and Frederick William I.[2]

All over Europe, below the kings, or at the head of affairs in the republics, were the aristocracies, graded downwards from the dukes who were official cousins of the kings, through various ranks down to the lesser nobility who were called gentry in England. They differed in accordance

---

[1] See, however, C. Picavet, *La diplomatie française au temps de Louis XIV* (1930), for an account of the true relation between that king as a person and the great administrative and diplomatic organization over which he presided. Other kings, *mutatis mutandis*, were similarly trammelled.

[2] *The Military Revolution*, p. 20.

with the diversity of social conditions of every kind from one kingdom or province to another. The Prussian Junkers were still peaceable, and even pacifist, working landlords. Although Bavaria had the first standing army in Germany after the Habsburgs, few of its nobility took up a military career, perhaps because church preferments provided a livelihood for younger sons; but it was the same in Protestant Württemberg. In several countries, however, the nobility had a military tradition. They no longer automatically incurred military duties and responsibilities, but they had a right to military commands. They were the men who fought duels and set store by the laws of honour. Most people believed that heredity made better soldiers; there were other currents of opinion, and Juvenal's caustic 'virtus vera nobilitas' was known as a family motto, but the common presumption was that in action and in word the man of good birth was more reliable. This was perhaps more true of France than of any other country. At the siege of the Huguenot fortress of Montpellier the young Puységur made a daring reconnaissance of a new hornwork which the defenders had built. He was taken to report to King Louis XIII in person. The king's first question was 'What is your name and what company are you in?' and his second 'si j'étois gentilhomme?'[1] The kings relied on the courage, the sense of honour, the loyalty and the veracity of this class. Their personal allegiance was one of the foundations of public order. As an illustration I will quote the sentences in which Matthew Wren, then bishop of Ely, threw the blame

---

[1] J. de Chastenet, marquis de Puységur, *Mémoires* (1690), p. 26. He belonged to the company of Carbon de Castel Jaloux, known to us from Rostand's play, *Cyrano de Bergerac*.

for the English Civil War on King James I. I do not think he was right, but in a muddled way he did appreciate the weight of an armed governing class in a turbulent society. After referring to the spirit of disorder and sedition in religion, to the ambition of the opposition leaders, and to James's favouritism to the Scots and jealousy of some of the ancient nobility, he went on: 'But the most mortal errour was that, the King committed in wholly disarming the nation.... To this end he courted the amity of all his neighbours, though upon most ignominious terms; he discountenanced all men of action; he advanced traffick and sought to introduce plenty, that by it he might the better immerse it in sloth and luxury.[1] But in this he was so unhappily fortunate, that the *English* gentry (anciently so renowned for their valour) are enervated with ease and debauchery, and are become both the prey and the scorn of the basest of the people.'[2]

Both the aristocracies and the soldiers had their own international connexions. This is not only true of those of the highest rank, such as Turenne who fought against his cousin William III, or Marlborough whose illegitimate nephew Berwick commanded the French forces in the Peninsula. It was true of all ranks, for they travelled, they learned languages, they learned all manner of things from allies and enemies. In their professional business the quicker

---

[1] This was a stock phrase of the moralists in accounting for defeat.

[2] 'Of the Origin and Progress of the Revolutions in England' in Gutch, *Collectanea curiosa*, I, 233–4. This was apparently written before the Restoration of Charles II. There were 'base' people who rose to high rank in the Puritan forces; but it may well be that the ideas of the 'Levellers' were essentially of civilian origin. Even the navy, which we should expect to have been more democratic than the army, was dissatisfied by the promotion of the upstart Rainboro.

they could imitate the best foreign models, the better for them, and there was a remarkable uniformity all over Europe in drill, in naval architecture, and no doubt in the manners and outlook of military, and even of naval, officers. This was not a negligible factor in the European consciousness. Warfare itself thus did something to draw the community together, and so did the diplomatic organization behind it. Negotiations were often obstructed by squabbles over etiquette and precedence. When there was a genuine desire to get on with the business these could be avoided, but I doubt whether this ever happened as smoothly and completely in any of the peace congresses as it did in the congresses of his allies which William III assembled at the Hague in the winters between his campaigns. Here the plenipotentiaries agreed to sit down in any order as they happened to come in.[1] At Ryswick, during the peace negotiation seven years later, there was a considerable fuss about the order of sitting at the table.[2]

The military revolution altered the military ways of the governing classes much as it altered the military ways of the Continent in general. It made them more regular and more subject to state control. A standing army or navy with an organized system of ranks offered a professional career. In every country this affected the lives of younger sons. In England it tended to separate the gentry from the business classes, because it provided an alternative to apprenticeship in the provincial towns or in the city of London. It had in a minor degree the effect which it had very markedly in

[1] Dispatch of Lord Dursley to the Earl of Nottingham, 24 April/25 March 1690, State Papers (Foreign), 84/222.
[2] *Actes et mémoires de la paix de Ryswick* (1725), II, 'Avertissement' and p. 19.

France and Brandenburg, of making country landowners familiar with military standards. Here again, however, we have to rely in most countries on social history of the impressionist kind; we still need surveys and statistics. This is far more so when we go down to the bottom of the scale, and here, because of the poverty of our literary sources, we are further from having any psychological insight into individual lives. We know in a general way where the military and naval recruits came from, and it seems to be true that in almost every country throughout the century it was exceptional for any but the poorest and least skilled elements of the population to be drawn upon. We know how it was that sturdy peasants left the farms in Sweden and Switzerland, and we chance to know from a speech of Oliver Cromwell how the New Model Army came to be manned, not by 'old decayed serving-men, tapsters and such kind of fellows', but by men that 'made some conscience of what they did'.[1] We know that in the second half of the century the social status, and the social provenance, of the cavalry trooper was declining. We do not know, however, whether recruiting was affected by the increase, where there was an increase, of the wage-earning workers, especially in the towns. Perhaps the greatest gap in our knowledge is about the means by which the ferocious discipline of the times transformed the recruits into the steady troops and ratings of the fighting services. Service tradition, care for the soldier's welfare, even patriotic feeling, were not highly developed; leadership and courage counted for more. Nor must we forget that there were other inherited military

[1] Speech of 13 April 1657. The Protector speaks of the Royalists as 'gentlemen, that have honour and courage and resolution in them', in the manner of his time.

7-2

traditions besides the royal and aristocratic tradition which led an articulated society into action as a whole. There was the old, honourable soldierly pride of the mercenary, and there was the newer, but well-established, tradition of the disciplined armies which fought for religion and national and constitutional freedom.

The consolidation of state sovereignty went hand-in-hand, as we saw, with firmer state control over the beginning, prosecution and winding-up of wars. They approximated more to the character of contests between communities directed into and through them by States. We often hear it said that the existence of separate national sovereignties in our own time is a cause, or a condition favourable to the causation, of wars. The rise of sovereignties should show what truth there may be in this. It would be useful if we could know whether Europe became more or less warlike in the period. Unfortunately we do not know. Perhaps the question is too vague if it is expressed in these general terms; but it would be useful if we could compare, for each year, for each State and for various combinations of years and States, the amount of money spent on warlike purposes, the amount of ammunition made and expended, the numbers killed, wounded and dead of wounds and disease, and many other figures of less close relevance.[1]

We cannot compare a Europe divided between sovereign territorial States with a unified or federal Europe, but we can compare the late seventeenth-century Continent with the Europe of the earlier period when sovereignties were not so

---

[1] My own guess is that the pressure of war on society became more severe, but the available information, as summarized in G. Bodart, *Losses of Life in Modern Wars* (1916), is very scanty.

completely exclusive in their claims over territory, that is, when they could overlap geographically, and when they were not so successful in controlling the lives of their populations. It may be paradoxical but it is true that the States of Europe were engaged in the task of world government. The world is governed and it was governed then. It was very badly governed, and besides misgovernment it suffered from lack of governance; but it was not anarchic. There were some regularities, such as good faith in contracts, which were understood and commonly respected over even wider areas than those of mature civilizations. Under their protection interdependence had grown up, fruitful exchanges of goods and knowledge and beliefs. We have seen that the wars were fought within a Europe of which the different regions depended on one another for the power to fight, or rather within a world-wide system of economic interdependence over which European traders and government exercised some control. It was a commonplace to say that 'God has ordained for the mutual commodity of man that the superfluities of one kingdom should supply the deficiencies of another'.[1] To say that States were interdependent means that none of them was absolutely free to act as it wished in relation to others, and none had absolute control over its own internal affairs. Any plan that it made for itself was to some extent a plan for the rest. The States of Europe had so much in common that they were aware of this in many of their dealings with one another. In economic affairs they knew that the exercise of sovereignty,

---

[1] Memorandum of English origin, 1603–4: for references to this and other English and French examples see p. 29 of part II, no. 10, in the Appendix (below p. 152), and Heckscher, *Mercantilism*, II, 278–80.

even in some of its oldest preserves such as the regulation of currency, affected the trade of other countries, and not only those which were their immediate customers and competitors. The rulers believed themselves to be responsible for the welfare of their own subjects, and they believed that no one else was responsible for it; but, in spite of constant disagreements and frequent conflicts, they co-operated with other States, and their co-operation was rooted in spontaneous co-operation between their subjects which they could facilitate or interrupt. In these senses they were actually engaged in the daily tasks of world government.

Only a few men, such as Grotius, believed that there was a community of legal rights as wide as the human race; but it is plain that there was in existence the framework of such a community. The sovereign States were relatively united and more active communities within this inchoate community. Some international communities were gathering strength and others were losing it, but the most noticeable change in the distribution of power was that the States were growing stronger. They made treaties with one another and less solemn agreements with other bodies which were not States, and the scores of treaties by which at any given moment a State was bound settled its place in the world, in the common organization such as it was. But its place in that interdependent world was defined not only by its treaties and the international diplomacy which preceded and followed them; many acts of state which in legal theory were of purely internal import did in fact affect the lives of men in other States, the interests of other parts of the world. So did many acts done by bodies within the State, by trading companies, by individual merchants or manufacturers, by

heresiarchs or professors. As a State tightened its control
over its citizens, it brought their affairs into the scope of its
own international proceedings.

This means that international relations of all kinds became
more orderly. At the beginning of the period loyalties were
often to ideas or to men, not to States, and both the ideas and
the men were often international. At the end the conflicting
forces of the mêlée were to a great extent polarized about the
States. The effect of this appears most clearly in the commercial and colonial questions to which I have already
referred. Of all the negotiations which decided such questions none involved greater issues than those over the
Spanish Succession in 1698 to 1700. They ended in failure.
When they broke down, a war began which was more
widespread, more desperate and more ruinous than any that
had ever been known. But if they are compared with the
negotiations of the Spaniards, the Dutch, the French and the
English over the same matters from the truce of 1609 to the
Treaty of Westminster in 1654, these negotiations will be
seen to show an improvement in the government of the
world. The partition treaties of 1698 and 1699 were made
between responsible authorities who knew what was at
stake. They had commercial statistics and reliable maps.
They were not at the mercy of uncontrollable frontiersmen.
In spite of all their vices and weaknesses they tried in good
faith to reach a settlement by mutual concessions, and they
were in a position to make good their promises. It was not
the diplomatists who failed, but the social organization
which they had inherited. The death of a boy in Bavaria, the
obstinacy of the Spanish grandees were too much for them.
The promise of that moment was not fulfilled; but the

efforts which ended thus in failure had not been wasted. The statesmen had gone far towards establishing public monopolies of force and a reliable machinery of diplomatic intercourse between the monopolists. They had done something in spite of themselves to realize the ideal of Pascal that the strong might be just and the just strong. And Pascal's phrase only reasserts, with a stronger emphasis on the paradox which it embodies in a world of imperfect human nature, the ideal of a just war.

I have outlined some of the arguments for three conclusions about war and society in the seventeenth century. My fourth arises from a general review of the whole matter, and I will give it in the words of a great historian. When William Stubbs reached the conclusion of his medieval *Constitutional History of England*, he permitted himself some general reflexions on the subject of conflict in history. In these pages he reviewed the wars of England in the seventeenth century as well as the Middle Ages. He used language which may not be acceptable to present-day historians, for he thought primarily of the 'great leaders'; but his thoughts can be transposed into our more democratic forms, and he is nearer to us than are some of his contemporaries, for he did not assume that on the human plane our history obeys any self-guaranteeing law of progress. He wrote: 'Their blows fell at random: men perished in arms against one another whose hearts were set on the same end and aim; and that good end and aim which neither of them had seen clearly was the inheritance they left to their children, made possible and realized not so much by the victory of one as by the truth and self-sacrifice of both.'

CHAPTER V

THE BARBARY CORSAIRS IN THE SEVENTEENTH CENTURY[1]

I N climate and physical geography, and also in the ways of life of its coasts and of the mountains and valleys behind them, the Mediterranean region is one whole.[2] Its historical diversities are like the play of coloured lights on a solid surface; but the seventeenth century was one of twelve during which its northern and southern shores were in the hands of two separate and inimical civilizations, different in religion, morals, law, economy and knowledge. The sea was nevertheless a busy highway. The Levant trade, the most important of all the French and the Italians, was also important for the English and the Dutch; but North Africa, from the Atlantic coast of Morocco to the Libyan desert, Barbary *par excellence*, was outside the European system of international law and conduct. Even when they were nominally at peace the Christians and the Moslems never trusted one another or succeeded for long in abiding by the rules on which they agreed. Both sides tried to enforce such rules by collective and vicarious punishments, by reprisals and by other devices to which men resort when there is no law between them. Each side, sometimes in spite of express treaty stipulations, made slaves of prisoners from the other: the Islamic society

---

[1] Originally published in *The Cambridge Historical Journal*, VIII (1944), no. 1.

[2] This is admirably shown throughout the well-known book of F. Braudel, *La Mediterranée et le monde méditerranéen à l'époque de Philippe II* (1949). A corrective to the bias against Islam shown by most of the nineteenth-century, especially the French, writers on this subject may be found in a popular book, P. Hubac, *Les barbaresques* (1949).

was based on slavery, and the Latin states also manned their war-galleys partly with their own criminals but largely with Moslems captured at sea.[1] To the seafaring men of Europe captivity in Barbary was a danger worse than shipwreck. It is indeed true that the Christian slave was an asset to his Moorish or Turkish master and so was worth preserving in good condition; the life of the domestic slave was not always intolerable, and he went to the hard labour of the quarries or the galleys only occasionally; but captivity in Barbary deserved its evil reputation. The novelists sometimes dispatched their least fortunate characters to the *bagnes* of the North African towns. The story of the prisoner escaped from the Moors is one of the most moving parts of Don Quixote: Cervantes had himself been a slave for five years in Algiers. Robinson Crusoe in his early days had a similar experience in Salee, and Defoe was one of the many economic writers who vainly urged that the Powers should unite to clean up this region.[2]

The redemption of captives was a favourite object of philanthropy. In England, especially under puritan influences, it occasioned many collections in the churches, and many charitable bequests. In catholic Europe the good work had a more continuous organization. At Meknes, the ordinary residence of the Moroccan sherifs, there was a hospital of Recollects supported by the kings of Spain for the benefit of slaves. Two orders of medieval origin devoted

[1] Slave-hunting was recommended by Monson to the Privy Council in 1620 as a method of financing war and was included in Allen's instructions in 1669: R. L. Playfair, *The Scourge of Christendom* (1884), pp. 37, 100. In spite of its unpromising title this is the best English book on Algiers.

[2] *A Plan of the English Commerce* (1728), part III, cap. 2. Within a few years after this date the Salee men were no longer a danger. *Robinson Crusoe* was published in 1719.

themselves especially to raising funds for ransoming slaves.[1] One of the great men of the seventeenth century, St Vincent de Paul, applied his remarkable abilities to the North African problem.[2] Finding that little was to be hoped for from the action of the French Crown, he made it one of the purposes of his new order, the Lazarists, not only to redeem captives, but also to succour those for whom no ransoms were forthcoming and to confirm them in the faith. He was faced by all the difficulties of those who try to alleviate what they cannot cure. He acquired for the Lazarists the right to provide the French consuls in Algiers, which they did for rather more than twenty years, devotedly trying to humanize the relations of the Moslems and the Christians; but it was the first duty of consuls to promote French commerce, and it is not surprising that Colbert put an end to the arrangement.

North Africa was not merely a chain of traps into which Europeans might fall; the sea-rovers also hunted far from home. In 1617 the Algerines pillaged Madeira, taking off twelve hundred prisoners and much else, including the church bells. In 1631 they carried away the entire able-bodied population of the little port of Baltimore in County Cork. Three years later they kidnapped eight hundred victims in Iceland. In 1625 pirates from Salee made their appearance on the Newfoundland Banks and seized forty vessels of le Havre alone. When Richelieu was at the height of his power in France there were constant slave-raids on the coast of Provence as well as on those of Italy, Sardinia and

[1] The work of the Redemptorist Father P. Dan, *Histoire de Barbarie et de ses corsaires* (1637), though valuable for its information, is intended mainly as a plea for support in this work.

[2] For the very doubtful story that he was a slave in Tunis in 1605–7 and escaped, see P. Coste, *Life and Works of St Vincent de Paul*, 1 (1934), 26–42.

Spain. In the early years of Charles I of England the corsairs held the Cornish coast in constant anxiety.[1] No wonder the first ship money writ gives as one of its purposes that the attacks of these enemies of the Christian name should be 'more manly met withal'. It was unfair of the Long Parliament, after anulling the ship-money proceedings, to go on in another Act[2] to blame Charles I's advisers for not using the proceeds of the customs to protect shipping against those of 'Argier' and others. The Act indeed added one per cent for three years to all the customs duties for this very purpose; but the Civil War broke out before anything came of it. Even in the days of James II and Pepys half a dozen Algerines together might be seen off the Dutch coast. As everyone knows these evils were not cured until the French conquered Algiers in 1830.

By European standards these States were small and weak. They exercised some degree of control over the inland pastoral tribes, and they had an export trade in corn, mainly carried in European vessels, which might be important to European States in times of scarcity or war; but in quantity this, and their other exports such as fruit, never compared with those of the Latin and northern countries. They had no industry worth mentioning; indeed, they had no serious 'war-potential' at all. They did not, to be sure, threaten the independence of European States, and they never stopped the Levant trade altogether, but they constantly molested it and probably somewhat restricted its development.[3] How was it possible for them, century after century, to plunder

[2] See M. Oppenheim in *Victoria County History, Cornwall*, 1 (1906), 495.
16 Car. I, c. 24. See also Grand Remonstrance, cl. 20.
[3] See, for instance, A. C. Wood, *History of the Levant Company* (1935), for the English experience.

the commerce and evade or defy the navies of the most powerful states of Europe?

At the beginning of the seventeenth century their history had recently entered on a new phase. In the Middle Ages their inhabitants had been landsmen; but when Ferdinand and Isabella had completed the reconquest of Spain, and it looked for a time as if Spain and Portugal would make still more extensive conquests, North Africa was saved by sea-power which enabled the land-forces of the Ottoman Empire to operate there. The beys who ruled in Algiers gained the support of Turkish janissaries by becoming vassals of the sultan. At sea they carried on what was from their point of view a *jihad*, a Holy War, and in the time of Francis I they benefited from his Turkish alliance, using the French ports as bases and sailing in concert with French fleets. This was the golden age of the corsairs. They frustrated the attempts of Charles V and Philip II to establish themselves on the North African shore or to rule the interior through puppet kings. They recovered Tunis and Tripoli. Farther west about 1550 the Moors, stimulated by Portuguese attacks as the Algerines had been by Spanish, formed the Sherifian empire, independent of the Porte, against which it set up a rival claim to the khalifate. It seemed as if the growing power of the beys might render them equally independent of the Porte. The sultans had reason for anxiety, for the battle of Lepanto in 1571 so broke their naval power that they were now confined to the eastern Mediterranean. Lepanto did not end the great days of the corsairs, but it weakened the authority of the sultans over them, and the sultans themselves completed this process by an ill-judged attempt to preserve their authority. In 1587 they decided that, in place of the beys, appointed for life, Algiers, Tunis and Tripoli were to be governed by triennial pashas. The effect of this measure was not perhaps to create three virtually independent pirate republics but to enable the three cities to use their privateers independently and with powerful effect.

The period which followed has been called the mercantile period of piracy in these three states. They lived by preying upon the commerce of Christendom,[1] and no authority that was ever set up in them could maintain itself unless it complied with the wishes of the janissaries and the corporations of sea captains. They were the most remarkable examples of pirate states, though not the only ones, for there were others, such as the Uscocchi of the Adriatic, not to mention the pirate communities of Madagascar or the Caribbean. The crowded and chaotic annals of these *magna latrocinia*, at least as they have been written by western historians, are an indescribable succession of military mutinies, civilian conspiracies, rebellions, civil wars, massacres, executions, torturings and assassinations. They had indeed some continuity of administration and of written records, and trade generally moved steadily enough along the caravan routes inland; but in the seaports rulers and ruled are said to have been equally cruel and capricious, equally extortionate and corrupt. The hundreds of treaties which they made were little better than waste paper. If their forces were under effective discipline it was discipline of an Oriental, not a European, type. Even when the constituted authorities wished it, which was not

[1] An authoritative statement on this point is that of Grotius, *De iure belli ac pacis*, III, ix, xix, where a French judgement on goods recaptured from the Algerines is discussed.

always the case, they were sometimes unable to make the rovers behave otherwise in peace than in war. The divan of Algiers wrote to Louis XIV: 'If we had the good fortune to enjoy such obedience as Your Majesty has from his subjects, we would not withhold anything that could afford him pleasure.'[1]

If the Sublime Porte had not existed these States, lacking its direct military support and the indirect support of its armies on the Danube, might have been crushed. Their major diplomatic relations, with such details as the admission of consuls in their territories, were dealt with in Constantinople; but from the European point of view they counted as independent. European States sometimes prevailed upon the sultan to assert his authority by dismissing a pasha, or, as in 1629, by insisting on their concluding a treaty; he granted commercial capitulations for them; but sometimes he had to deal with the Barbary States as grasping and untrustworthy allies. In Tunis he was sometimes obeyed in the early part of the century, and in Tripoli his power lasted longer, but in 1714 even Tripoli expelled the janissaries. The fleets of the corsairs served the sultan as mercenaries in some of his wars, having, indeed, the inducement that the state of war frightened away the merchantmen and so interrupted their ordinary livelihood. In 1638 the Venetians defeated them soundly at Valona, but the sultan made peace before they could have their revenge and so forfeited their support. In 1640 they refused their help and the sultan failed in an attempt to punish them. In 1646 they co-operated again and in the next year they formed the vanguard of the fleet which

[1] Letter of 21 September 1686 in Plantet, *Correspondance des deys d'Alger avec la cour de France*, I (1889), 122.

the Venetians defeated at the Euboean channel. There were some occasions when they took part in the war of Candia (1648–69), but they did not co-operate effectively or give the Turks substantial help. So great was their independence of the Porte that they might have been expected to fall out with one another. In the sixteen-twenties there was, indeed, a four years' war between Algiers and Tunis, originating in tribal affairs inland, and the Porte was too weak to stop it. Again in 1630–46 the Algerine admiral Ali Bitchnin was ambitious to rule over the neighbouring pashaliks; but on the whole their aggressive instincts turned only seawards.

Algiers was by far the strongest and most dangerous of them. Its population at its height is said to have varied between 100,000 and 150,000, besides some 10,000 Jews. There were perhaps 10,000 janissaries, hereditary professional soldiers serving for life, and the internal government was carried on in a tumultuary way as a virtual republic. Each of the ships carried a volunteer detachment of janissaries, and their strength lay in the size of their crews. They were mostly fitted out by co-operative groups of owners. Their one function was to prey upon commerce. The public finances depended mainly on the state's share of all prizes. The rest, in prescribed proportions, provided the livelihood of the owners, officers, soldiers and crew. The prisoners, whether for their labour or for their ransoms, were always an important part of the booty; the rest was handled mainly by the Jews, who could dispose of it anywhere from Leghorn to Amsterdam.[1]

---

[1] See H. I. Bloom, *Economic Activities of the Jews of Amsterdam in the Seventeenth and Eighteenth Centuries* (1937), pp. 75–82.

Tunis was less formidable than Algiers, less unsettled in its politics and more given to peaceful commerce; there the *reïs* or corporation of sea captains had no political influence; but Tunis was never negligible. Tripoli was still weaker and it was more subject to the sultan, but its position, far from any naval base open to the French, made it dangerous to their commerce. Its fleet suffered in the sixteen-thirties at the hands of the knights of Malta, but in and after the time of Colbert it was Tripoli that did the greatest damage to French commerce. Salee, close to the modern Rabat, owed its rise to the expulsion of the Moriscoes from Spain in 1609, and its hunting grounds were mainly in the Atlantic. Altogether it has been calculated that in the first half of the seventeenth century, the period of their greatest power, the four pirate states mustered some 150 ships with a thousand guns and a complement of 20,000 men.

In one respect indeed the Barbary States were by no means so feeble as they appeared. They were not mere outposts of Islamic civilization: they also represented the backwash of European energy as it beat against the African shore. First the men were largely Europeans. It is sometimes said that in Algiers the overwhelming majority of the *reïs* were rene-gades. This would be hard to prove, but it seems to be true of most of those whose names are prominent.[1] There were also at times Christians who served there (as sailors only) without being converted. In 1609, for instance, the leaders of the Tunisian fleet were Ward, Bishop, Sir Francis Verney and Kara Osman. The Turks did not press their slaves to

---

[1] O. de Haedo, *Topographia e historia general de Argel* (1612), f. 18, gives a list of the captains of galiots in 1581: out of thirty-five, twenty-three were rene-gades, one a renegade's son and one a Jew.

become Moslems: those who did so became free men, to their owners' loss;[1] but thousands chose this way of improving their material lot. In 1629–34 out of 1331 Frenchmen made captive 149 renegued. Perhaps the renegades were not all absolute villains. The French at least alleged that some of them were useful agents for Great Britain, such as an English queen of Muley Ismail, the Moroccan counterpart of Louis XIV, or the Huguenot refugee Pillet, who served under William III in Ireland before he became governor of Salee.

The Barbary corsairs not only included men of European race, they also practised the European art of naval warfare. Early in the seventeenth century they gained an advantage by introducing the sailing broadside ship into the Mediterranean and so ending the era when there were no fighting ships there except galleys. They owed this advantage, decisive until the Christians followed the example, to the Englishman Ward, who taught sailing at Tunis, and the Dutchman Simon Danzer, who soon followed at Algiers. Probably there were instructors and experts of other kinds. Most of the artificers in Algiers in the late sixteenth century were renegades, and for some time after that the efficiency of their shipbuilding was due to renegades and even to hired European workmen. It is scarcely credible that the great mole of Algiers was made by anyone except first-rate European engineers. Most astonishing of all is the fact that until about 1700 most of their artillery was cast in Christendom. Thence came many musket-locks and at least a great part of their gunpowder. English lead

[1] In Morocco their status became better but they remained slaves: Pidou de St Olon, *Relation de l'empire du Maroc* (1695), p. 77.

went into their bullets. Some of these munitions were captured; but by far the greater part were bought. The secret of their power therefore lies in the character of their relations with the Christian States and Christian traders.

At the beginning of the century the Spaniards and the Portuguese had no longer any hope of settling the North African question once and for all by invasion. That, the only thorough solution, was never undertaken between the great Portuguese defeat of Alcassar in 1578 and the French conquest of Algiers in 1830. The Spaniards, indeed, still held Melilla, Ceuta, Larache, Mamora, Oran and Mars el Kebir, besides Sicily, which was an admirable base; but they were too weak to make a full use of these posts, and the knights of Malta, like the Venetians, were mainly concerned to keep back the Turkish forces east of the Sicilian narrows. The Portuguese had Mazagan and Tangier. The French had a trading post or factory to the east of La Calle, with the high-sounding name of 'le Bastion de France', and another in Tunisian territory at Cap Nègre, but these were never in any sense bases for warlike operations. The Europeans could use no means of coercion except the action of fleets without landings. They attacked the corsairs at sea and they made naval demonstrations, sometimes with the aim of obtaining treaties; but the results were poor. The last good chance in the galley era was thrown away when Gianandrea Doria led the fleets of Spain and the Italian cities to failure in 1601. Only two of the naval actions of the first half of the century can be called glorious, the destruction of the Tunisian fleet of more than thirty sail by the French in 1609 and the Venetian victory at Valona in 1638.

In 1616 Malherbe addressed the gallants who were about to start in one of the French expeditions:

> Tantôt nos navires, braves
> De la dépouille d'Alger,
> Viendront les Maures esclaves
> A Marseille décharger;
> Tantôt, riches de la perte
>
> De Tunis et de Biserte,
> Sur nos bords étaleront
> Le coton pris en leurs rives
> Que leurs pucelles captives
> En nos maisons fileront.[1]

But no such results followed in the ignominious event.

The first part of the century saw the greatest power of the corsairs because then the general state of Europe specially favoured them. The last quarter of the sixteenth century and the first half of the seventeenth formed the worst period in all modern history for the policing of the seas. Lepanto not only pushed the Turks back into the eastern Mediterranean; it was followed by a general decline of the navies of the Italian states. The Dutch and Elizabethan wars crippled the Spanish navy, and the wars of religion the French: when Henry IV decided to fight the Tunisians in 1609 his fleet consisted of one Dutch-built ship. Meanwhile King James I was letting Queen Elizabeth's ships rot at their moorings and Englishmen with a thirst for nautical adventure were unable to assuage it in the navy. Captain Henry Mainwaring, a member of one of the best families in Cheshire, set up a Barbary state of his own at Mehdia just north of Salee, whence forty sail of English pirates with two thousand men

[1] This fragment is included in the collections of Malherbe's poems: I take the dating from la Roncière.

cruised for three or four years in two main squadrons under Sir John Fearne and Captain Peter Croston.[1] Naval warfare even in the Channel and the North Sea at this time was not much better than a succession of confused encounters between armed merchantmen and privateers under no effective control by their States.

Even with their scanty naval forces the Christian States could, however, easily have mastered Barbary if they had steadily acted together, as in the early years of the century they sometimes did. When Franco-Spanish rivalry was suspended by the Treaty of le Cateau Cambrésis in 1559, for the time being the French alliance with the corsairs came to an end. When the Tunisian fleet was beaten in 1609 there were French and Spanish ships in the victorious force, and the Englishman Sir Anthony Shirley was on board. Within a very few years however, any proposal for joint action was regarded with suspicion. Even at that time Henry IV was thinking of renewing the alliance with the corsairs, and of stirring up a revolt of the Moriscoes: only his assassination put a stop to these plans. The strange persistence of the French in their unprofitable North African trade cannot be fully explained on economic grounds: the government backed up the merchants of Languedoc and Provence because it hoped to get political influence or power through them.[2] Spain often feared that an alliance might come about between the

[1] Sir Julian Corbett, *England in the Mediterranean*, 2nd ed. 1 (1917), 50–2.

[2] For an emphatic statement of this view see H. D. de Grammont, *Histoire d'Alger* (1887), pp. 197–8. The history of the French trading establishments is given fully in P. Masson, *Histoire des établissements et du commerce français dans l'Afrique barbaresque* (1903), which has an excellent bibliography. The same writer's works, the *Histoire du commerce français dans le Levant au XVIIe siècle* 1896) and *Histoire du commerce français dans le Levant au XVIIIe siécle* (1911), are important for the corsairs.

corsairs and the English or Dutch or both. The Spaniards did indeed act now and again with the Dutch, and when Sir Robert Mansell appeared off Algiers in 1622 he had both Dutch and Spanish ships in company; but the Spaniards were there less to support him than to watch him, and, if we are to believe Sir Julian Corbett, they had good reason for their suspicions. Charles I of England angled for North African help in his war against Spain. From the time when the Dutch became involved in the Thirty Years War there was no co-operation between the Mediterranean and the North Sea powers.

Another and a more subtle weakness on the European side arose from commerce. Not one of the Christian powers maintained an attitude of unmitigated hostility to the Barbary states. Spain had a clear record: until the reign of Charles III she remained on religious grounds nominally at war with them, and she discouraged all kinds of intercourse. But even Spain could not do without their trade entirely; she wanted some of their commodities, among others wax for church candles, and these she bought mainly from French intermediaries. Nor is it cynical to say that the astuteness of the French and the English did more than Spanish aversion to prevent any reconciliation with the Moslems. The French went on trading with them all through the century in spite of many disappointments. The trade never amounted to much: the quantities of fish and coral from the coast, the corn, wool, Morocco leather, hides, oil, old copper and horses from inland never justified the expense of the quarrels they led to. In 1628 Richelieu agreed to a treaty in which perhaps the interests and certainly the pride of France were sacrificed to those of the Bastion. The

Bastion was thrice destroyed and thrice restored; there were moments when the prospects looked good, but none of the successive French companies had more than an ephemeral success, and most of the shareholders lost their money. The French, which in the main meant the Marseillais, were very jealous of the trade of other nations. They aimed indeed at a monopoly of trade with North Africa for their flag if not for their own merchants. The most famous French trader of the century, the Corsican Sanson Napollon, was killed in an attack on Tabarkah, which the Genoese had held since 1540.

About the middle of the century there were changes in Europe which at last made it possible for the Christian states to take effective action. The rise of the British and Dutch fleets began a consolidation of maritime power.[1] After the first Anglo-Dutch war Blake and then de Ruyter passed through the Straits with squadrons such as had never been seen there before. Within a few years Colbert provided France with a navy. The corsairs tried to meet these forces by cruising always in squadrons; but the pressure of the three great naval and trading states gradually wore down their strength. The population of Algiers and the number of its janissaries began to decline. It underwent two internal revolutions which were evidently due to the sinking fortunes of the wars on commerce.[2] In 1659 the presidency of the divan

[1] The history of French naval operations is narrated fairly fully by C. de la Roncière, *Histoire de la marine française*, IV–VI (1910–32); Sir Julian Corbett, *England in the Mediterranean*, 2nd ed., 2 vols. (1917), is more concerned with strategic questions, and the treatment of C. de Jonge, *Geschiedenis van het nederlandsche zeewesen*, 2nd ed., 6 vols. (1858–62), is comparatively brief.

[2] Did this in any way contribute to the change in Tunis by which from 1650 the deys made their office hereditary and autocratic though still requiring confirmation from the Porte? There are unfortunately no reports from French representatives in Tunis between 1641 and 1660 in *Correspondance des deys de Tunis et des consuls de France*, ed. E. Plantet, I (1893).

was taken from the pashas and given to elected aghas or military officers. It was intended that each of these should hold office only for two months. In fact only five aghas held office until 1671, when this most anarchic phase of the constitution ended, and every one of these was murdered. They were followed by elective deys, of whom the first four were corsair captains. In theory the deys were despots; the power of the divan was now merely nominal; but the dey was a prisoner in his undefended palace, and if he displeased the soldiers or the seamen he was promptly murdered, a fate which overtook more than one of the holders of the office between 1671 and 1701. In 1704 the Porte resigned itself to this state of things and in 1711 the pashas were abolished.

Although the European navies acted more powerfully, their objectives were still limited. From time to time the ports were blockaded; convoys were provided for the merchantmen, which did not always appreciate the favour,[1] and, as before, there were naval demonstrations. The Dutch never did more than attack the corsairs at sea, though sometimes the Barbary states gave way to their demands for fear that they would do more. The French and the British tried to establish fresh bases on African soil. The French made their attempt at Jigelli in 1671; but after holding it for three months they were driven out. This ill-starred expedition was the French retort to the best of all the efforts made by Europeans in the seventeenth century on North African soil, the British occupation of Tangier. The British, it is true, did

---

[1] For the failure of Colbert's convoy system see C. W. Cole, *Colbert*, I (1939), 388 ff. Convoyed ships were not liable to be searched, and this was an advantage in commercial competition; for this reason the duke of York provided convoys in 1662: see A. C. Wood, *History of the Levant Company* (1935), pp. 212–13.

not have the task of conquering their foothold; it was handed over by the Portuguese; but they held it for more than twenty years against the attacks of the Moors; they built up its trade, and they employed the best engineers of England and Italy in constructing its mole. It was in England, not in Africa, that the Tangier adventure failed. Unfortunately, like all the others, it did fail.[1]

In addition to these more ambitious attempts against the Barbary corsairs, British and French admirals from time to time blockaded their harbours and cannonaded their towns: Blake poured shot into Tunisian Porto Farina and Sandwich into Algiers; Spragge cut through the boom of Bugia Bay and destroyed seven Algerine frigates there. Narborough accounted for four ships in the harbour of Tripoli and a good many more Algerines. Herbert, who succeeded to Narborough's command, took part in defending Algiers against the Moors and then fought against it, finally making a treaty which lasted, with little modification, for about a century. Under Louis XIV the French tried their hand, and they were the first to throw in not mere cannon-balls but explosive shells. The bomb-ketch was a new invention in 1683 and 1688, when they used it with destructive effect against Algiers. On the second occasion the dey threatened that as soon as the first shell was fired the French consul would be blown from the cannon's mouth. He made good his threat, and massacred thirty-nine other French denizens as well. 'It is not because you are at war with us,' he scribbled

---

[1] Tangier had to resist the Moors at a time when Morocco, in spite of internal divisions, was full of vigour. Muley Ismail, with French support, took the Spanish port of Mamora in the year after Tangier was evacuated and in 1689 Larache on the Atlantic coast. He began the twenty-six years siege of Ceuta, which was not raised till 1720.

on the back of the French ultimatum, 'it is because you fire bombs. If you are strong enough, come on shore, or fire at the ships.'[1] After the bombardments the French commanders, Tourville and d'Estrées, triumphantly announced that the infidels had been chastised; but the effect was only momentary. Their insolence revived at least as soon as the fleets weighed anchor.[2]

Like French merchants in some of the other places to whom Louis XIV extended an unsought and provocative protection, the traders in North Africa would have preferred to be left alone. Denis Dusault, the best of the commercial negotiators whom Louis employed in Algiers, expressed this view. He disapproved of the bombardment of 1683 because it interrupted commerce and threw the Algerines into the arms of the English and Dutch. At least one judicious modern French writer takes the same view: the bombardments contributed to the restoration of peace, but there is nothing to prove that the same result might not have been got without them more cheaply and without any atrocities against French subjects.[3] Sometimes it was the same with the English: in 1677 the British consul in Algiers wrote that war was being maintained without sufficient reason: he could have obtained satisfaction for all the grievances.[4]

In this first phase after the rise of the navies there was some improvement in the attempt to establish a regime of law. The treaties with the Barbary states, though they were still

[1] Plantet, *Correspondance Alger*, I, 158.
[2] In 1682 the sultan refused to help Algiers against Duquesne: this alienated Algiers, which in 1689 refused to receive a pasha sent at the instance of France.
[3] A. Boutin, *Les Traités de paix et de commerce de la France avec la Barbarie* (1902), p. 530.
[4] Playfair, *op. cit.* p. 125.

often disregarded on both sides, showed some approach to laying down rules which could be enforced in the actual circumstances. The Christian jurists and diplomatists were still, however, confused and uncertain as to what sort of equilibrium they wanted to establish, what sort of relations they should regard as normal. Rules were laid down for the examination of ships' papers, for the definition of contraband and so on, resembling those in force between the Christian states but adapted to the special circumstances. France seems to have led the way in bringing in the system of Mediterranean passes, the Dutch and the English following.[1] In subsequent treaties this system was extended to the outer seas, the corsairs always undertaking to observe certain restraints. Their position was strong because all these treaties were one-sided: they restricted the rights of the Barbary corsairs to pillage European commerce, but the corsairs had no commerce of their own for the Europeans to pillage in reprisal. Moreover, international law gave a new respectability to their enterprises. Although they all flew the same green flag sown with stars, they made war and peace separately. They were four, not one, so when one was at war with a European state it could offer a convenient alibi to ships of the others, thus enabling them to join in the forays without breaking the peace. In the same way, the European states also were many, not one, so if one of them was at war with a Barbary state the rest were neutrals, and the rights of a belligerent afforded welcome opportunities of getting on board neutral vessels. 'It was always easy to visit a vessel,

[1] The history of Dutch Mediterranean passes is traced in F. J. W. H. Sandbergen, *Nederlandsche en nederlandsch-indische scheepsnationaliteit* (s.a. ? 1932). Similar information on British and French passes seems not to be readily available.

destroy her pass and declare she had none, a course which was habitually adopted.'[1] On the other hand, the European merchants were not blameless. 'It is but fair to state that most of the English captives were people who had brought this misfortune on themselves by serving on board vessels at enmity with Algiers or by not providing themselves with the necessary Mediterranean passes.'[2] Just as the merchants criticized the action of their states, the admirals and the statesmen on their side blamed the merchants. Herbert, the admiral, wrote from Algiers in 1681: 'I am very confident that His Majesty hath been twice, if not thrice, engaged in a war with these people by the misbehaviour of his consuls.' He recommended that £300 or £400 a year should be paid for 'a man of known integrity, capacity and courage, and of some fortune'.[3]

Never were the malpractices of the traders more evident than during the occupation of Tangier. When it was discovered that an English firm had been landing ammunition at Salee, Sir Palmes Fairborne, the governor, wrote: 'Whilst the enemy can be supplied with powder and other stores from England it will be impossible to reduce these people to any reason.'[4] But even in this vital matter British policy, like that of the Dutch and the French, conformed to the self-contradictory general situation. In 1682, towards the end of the Tangier days, a treaty with Morocco was concluded at Whitehall. Colonel Kirke, of Kirke's Lambs, had written from Tangier recommending that the king should indeed suppress the gun-runners, but only in order to nationalize

[1] Playfair, *op. cit.* p. 190. For an example, see the letter of Seignelay to the dey of Algiers, March 1685, in Plantet, *op. cit.* I, 112 ff.
[2] Playfair, *op. cit.* p. 136.   [3] *Ibid.* p. 137.
[4] Enid M. G. Routh, *Tangier* (1912), p. 185.

their business. His plan was that the Crown itself should sell the Moroccans contraband 'to a certain stint only', and he regarded this contraband trade as the best security for the observance of treaties of peace. The Crown adopted his advice, but with the difference that the Whitehall treaty gave the Moors an unlimited right to buy contraband in England. Their better behaviour was to be bought at a price which would make them dangerous in any event to the rest of Europe, and very likely to Great Britain as well. This was not an isolated or even an exceptional decision. It could be excused by the attitude of France and Holland.[1] In 1666, when these two were in alliance against Britain, Roland Fréjus made a treaty with Muley-Arxid, promising French support against rebels who were in alliance with the English. Tangier was the cause; powder and munitions were part of the bargain, and Algiers, Tunis and Tripoli were supposed to be aimed at from this new *point d'appui*.[2] A few years later the Algerines were allowed to use the arsenal at Toulon. The rivalries of the European States were so inveterate and had so come to dominate all other considerations that it was to them more than to anything else that the Barbary states owed their survival.

This was true not only of the supply of munitions but also on the plane of high politics. The possibility of international action was more remote than ever. When any state wanted to fit out a fleet for the Mediterranean, or even for service elsewhere, the standing answer to embarrassing questions

[1] In their treaty of 1662 the Dutch agreed to supply the Algerines with naval stores; in the subsequent period both they and the English seem to have sent considerable quantities of masts, spars, cordage, pitch, tar and sailcloth to North Africa.
[2] See his *Relation* (1670): there is an English translation of 1671.

about its purpose was to say that it was aimed against the Barbary pirates.[1] This excuse was put forward, for instance, even to explain the naval preparations of William III for his expedition against England; indeed it was so much a standard form of diplomatic politeness that it was used on that occasion by both sides. The letter in which James II expressed it is interesting, not only for its quiet irony, but also as a clear statement of the policy of the Algerines always to be at war at least with some of the European powers. On 15/25 May 1688 James wrote to his son-in-law: 'I am now setting out my summer guard, though there will be little for them to do, except the French who are gone, or going to Algiers, oblige these people to make peace with them, and then of course they must fall out with me, though they have already war with you.'[2]

This forecast, like some others made by James II, was not correct. As it turned out, Great Britain never had a formal war with Algiers from 1682 to 1816, when Lord Exmouth gave it its last British bombardment. The reason was that the train of events which began with William's expedition against England brought another great change in the fortunes of North Africa. The Barbary states had already become participants in the European balance of power, and the diplomatic activity of 1688 was part of the preparation for the great wars of Louis XIV against the European coalition. The French got their peace with Algiers, and two years later they went further and began to invite the Algerines to act with them as co-belligerents. Pontchar-

---

[1] For earlier instances see Corbett, *op. cit.* I, 78–9, 100–1, 240.

[2] Sir James Dalrymple, *Memoirs of Great Britain and Ireland*, II (1773), App. pt. I, 291.

train, the minister of marine, came over to the point of view
of the merchants and inaugurated a new policy of concilia-
tion. He made a treaty which provided for every sort of
collaboration short of joint naval action. The French also
responded hopefully when Muley Ismail of Morocco in
1691 asked for a treaty after six years in which there had been
neither war nor peace. Nothing came of this: Muley Ismail
wanted Ceuta, and he refused to act against any other
North African state on grounds of religion, not receiving,
curiously enough, the answer that the same argument would
make it impossible for Louis to fight against Spain. The
French policy of appeasement was successful from the commercial point of view and it led to a long peace between
France and Algiers; but for the purpose of obtaining help in
in the European war it was a failure. It was the appearance
of Great Britain as a Mediterranean power in good earnest
which, more than anything else, marked a new stage in the
decline of the corsairs into insignificance.

After the French bombardments, a new series of land wars
had begun between Algiers and its neighbours. In 1687
came the first of a series of attacks on Oran which were
renewed every year until in 1708 it fell. From 1689 until his
assassination in 1695 the dey Chaban, in alliance with
Tripoli, made war on Morocco and Tunis. He was a violent
and ambitious warrior, and his aggressions were connected
with the European struggle; but in his time the dey could
no longer pay his troops from the prizes taken at sea and so
was forced to seek booty on land.

British sea-power in the Mediterranean increased step by
step. After La Hogue the French Levant trade was almost
extinguished. For the first time a British fleet wintered in the

Mediterranean, and it is not a coincidence that in the next year the fleets of Algiers, Tunis and Tripoli served under the sultan in the Black Sea. During the course of the war the corsairs still gave trouble: the existing British treaty with Tripoli was renewed and Tripoli was promised arms and ammunition for use against Tunis. The treaty with Algiers was renewed twice, and British relations with Tunis and Morocco were correspondingly bad. How far the French and British fomented these local quarrels and how far they merely took advantage of them it would be hard to determine; but in any case the successes of the maritime powers against France were reflected in their prestige with Chaban and perhaps in his victories. They also led to a great change in the nature of the fleets. The system of private ownership did not enable them to stand up against the growing strength of the European navies, and so they became state navies, with regular dockyards and gun foundries of their own.

All these tendencies went further during the war of the Spanish Succession. In 1702 or 1703, indeed, the supporters of the Habsburg claim to Spain—the king of Portugal, the prince of Hesse-Darmstadt and the admiral of Castile— negotiated for an alliance with Muley Ismail, and failed, as Louis XIV had failed, because his terms were too hard. They went so far as to ask for troops, as to which there is a gibe of Voltaire: in consequence of their failure 'les chrétiens se déchirèrent de leurs propres mains sans se joindre celles des barbares'.[1] But the allies did not need to bring the barbarians into Europe: their superiority was more manifest than in the previous war. The Dutch, indeed, had hostilities with Algiers in 1702 and in 1707–12, and had to pay a price

[1] *Siècle de Louis Quartorze*, cap. xviii.

for peace in the latter year, while France, conversely, had to renew the treaties with Tunis after incidents in 1710 and 1713; but the main fact is that each step in the advance of allied sea-power, Gibraltar, Vigo, Malaga, weakened not only France but the corsairs as well. There was no shipping now that offered valuable booty except that of the British and Dutch, but they suffered fewer losses than ever before. Gibraltar depended on Morocco for some of its supplies, and these were readily forthcoming. The land warfare in Africa went on. In 1701–8 Algiers successfully defended itself against Muley Ismail of Morocco and even captured Oran from the Spaniards. But this land warfare did not pay, and from 1708 there were thirty years of peace between the Barbary states. They fell back on the only resource left to them, the comparatively safe system of pillaging the commerce of the weaker European states or blackmailing those states, which by then included the Dutch, into buying them off with tributes.

Even after the war of the Spanish succession the Barbary states were a nuisance for more than a century. Their comparative weakness did not put an end to the need for redeeming captives. The divisions of Christendom still left the way open for them to do damage out of all proportion to their resources.

CHAPTER VI

THE CYCLE OF WAR AND PEACE
IN MODERN HISTORY

WHEN the Senate of the University of London invited me to deliver this lecture, I felt grateful not only for the honour that was done me, but also for so great an opportunity. Nowhere else can an English historian address such an audience as gathers annually on this occasion. I am glad also to pay my tribute to the greatness of Mandell Creighton as an historian. There are others who are better qualified than I am to praise his writings, but, when I became editor of the *English Historical Review* in succession to R. L. Poole, who had worked on it from its foundation in 1886, I learnt much which could not have been learnt in any other way about its first editor, Creighton. In particular, I learnt something of what he had done for the tone and temper of British historical studies, and those services cannot be rated too highly.

Honesty, indeed, compels me to admit that the subject I have chosen is not the sort of subject that Creighton ever studied himself, or encouraged anyone else to study. He was not a sociological historian; he did not believe in drawing lessons from history,[1] and he might well have considered this subject unprofitable or even boring. Yet I hope, before I have done, to cite his authority for that view of it which I intend to set before you.

My subject is one of those broad interpretative ideas

[1] Louise Creighton, *Life and Letters of Mandell Creighton*, II (1904), 504.

which attract others beside historical specialists, the idea that war and peace follow one another in a regular cycle. I do not intend to discuss whether or when we shall have another war, nor, more generally, what are the causes of war, but simply to examine the idea that the causes of war, whatever they may be, operate in this special way.

Many writers, of many schools, from the distant past to the present day, have held this idea, sometimes in isolation and sometimes as part of a wider system of thought. In all its different forms it asserts that during a state of peace there are conditions which necessarily lead to an outbreak of war, that during the ensuing war there are others which bring peace back again, and that the process, having returned to a point where it was before is, and presumably will be, repeated indefinitely. The question is, whether this idea is true.

Some of us, no doubt, would be disposed to answer summarily that it is only one of the many ideas which we call deterministic, and is therefore to be rejected on the strength of arguments which hold good against determinism as such, and by which the freedom of the human will is vindicated. That is my own opinion. I hold that it is permissible for a historian to reject either a particular or a general statement on the ground of antecedent improbability. Unless this were so we could not make our historical knowledge a part of a coherent body of knowledge about the world as a whole. What we admit as probable will indeed depend on our opinions about many matters outside what we ordinarily call history, on our philosophy, for instance, or our psychology or some other science, and, since opinion on these matters changes, our historical knowledge will partake of that provisional or hypothetical character to which natural science is content to limit its claims. There actually are some historical writers who deny that improbability makes a statement less credible; but I do not think we need take them seriously. It is not they who are troublesome nowadays, but the extremists who not only hold that we can dismiss some historical statements *a priori* as untrue, but go further, and maintain that we can know *a priori* that other historical statements must be true. They would make no difficulty about agreeing that the cycle of war and peace will be open to rejection on *a priori* grounds if such grounds can be established.

Unhappily we cannot assume that there is even an agreed starting-point for a discussion of determinism in general, but, for our present purpose, we may leave this prior question undecided. Even those of us who are least inclined to determinism must admit that there are some recurrences and regularities in the course of history. Every day the population of London goes through its cycle of movements from home to work and back again. Every year every kind of organized life in every country passes through movements which ultimately depend on the seasons and the annual motions of the solar system. We are accustomed to the idea of longer cycles in economic life, which may or may not be associated with the incidence of sun-spots. Historians in general believe that the whirligig of time brings in his revenges. Consequently, we may take it for granted that there are cycles in human life, and we may ask the question whether the alternations of peace and war, as historians actually have described them, do fall into the cyclical scheme of recurrence. It has been put in the form of a simple analogy. A field of corn goes through a cycle of growth and ripening entirely independent of the birds which lay their eggs and rear their young in it. When that cycle is completed, after the harvest, next year, punctually on the first of September, the partridge shooting will begin. Does war follow a cycle equally independent of our control?

As an approach to this question it will be convenient to consider one episode in the history of the idea, to trace it as it was expressed in a special form, almost a special formula, by three writers of the sixteenth and seventeenth centuries. I do not pretend that this is an important chapter in the history of ideas, but it is one of the lesser curiosities of literature, and, in addition to being serviceable as an illustration, it should have some value as a parable.

It begins with a sentence written by a minor historian in a country and a time of which Creighton had an intimate knowledge, Italy in the early sixteenth century. The historian is Luigi da Porto, who was also one of the chain of story-tellers who handed down to Shakespeare the story of Romeo and Juliet. Even now, when we have lived through so many upheavals, it is moving to read his simple story of the events of his early twenties. He tells us how the League of Cambray was formed, how it brought war to his native town of Vicenza, and how, a few months later, he commanded a company of light horse in the mountains of Friuli until he was struck down with a dangerous wound.[1] Before those days Vicenza had enjoyed a hundred years of peace. He describes its wealth and beauty, its gardens and palaces and fountains; he says that he feared it was in danger from

[1] *Lettere storiche*, ed. B. Bressan (1857). For his qualities as a writer see the brief characterization by C. Foligno in *Nuovo archivo veneto*, nuova serie, XXIII (1912), especially p. 7.

some influence of the stars, which are envious of such un-bounded enjoyment, and then comes the sentence to which I refer: 'I have always heard it said that peace brings riches; riches bring pride; pride brings anger; anger brings war; war brings poverty; poverty brings humanity; humanity brings peace; peace, as I have said, brings riches, and so the world's affairs go round.'[1]

Luigi da Porto was not a philosophical historian. Almost the whole of his little book consists of straightforward narratives of diplomatic and military occurrences, without discussion or speculation. When he does enunciate an idea he does not claim it as his own invention: the sentence that I have quoted begins with the words 'io sempre ho udito dire'. He does, indeed, allude from time to time to the superhuman entities which presided, as he and other good Catholics and believers in free will supposed, over all ter-restrial things. He says that fickle Fortune is the arbitress of human affairs; he glances at her outrages and her cruel mockery. He believes that every man has his lot from the day when he is born. He notices portents such as comets and the birth of monsters; he ascribes the fall of the Trojans, the Greeks and the Romans to the stars in their courses, and he fears the baleful star of Venice; but he does not try to bring all this into any close relation with his story, point by point. To tell the truth, he most commonly touches on these high matters to open or wind up a paragraph in a moderately elevated literary form.[2]

In this he is completely in contrast with a graver historian,

---

[1] Letter of 7 March 1509, *ibid.* p. 26. It must not be supposed that the letters were put into their final form at the ostensible dates. The verb which I translate 'brings' is, in each case, 'fa'.

[2] The best examples are on pp. 47, 53, 66, 79, 87, 114 and 209.

Michael von Aitzing,[1] who used the cycle, rather more than seventy years later, as the framework of one of his books. Whether he copied it directly or indirectly from Luigi da Porto, I cannot tell, but there are reasons for thinking that he may have done so.[2] Aitzing was an Austrian *Freiherr* who wrote many books in the course of his chequered career. He is chiefly remembered now because, we may say, he invented political journalism. He was the first of all men to publish periodical summaries of political news. They began as continuations of his books on contemporary history, and he wrote them regularly for sale at the Frankfurt spring and autumn fairs. He spent many years in the Low Countries, where at one time he was closely in touch with those Antwerp publishers and engravers who were famous for their illustrated books and atlases. When the revolt of the Netherlands against King Philip II of Spain made Antwerp unsafe, he lived in Cologne, as one of the Catholic exiles who congregated there. Amongst these exiles there was a group

---

[1] This way of writing his name seems to be the best among many variants from Aitsingerus to Eyzinger. There is a full account of him, with a bibliography, by F. Stieve in *Historische Classe der kön. bayer. Akademie der Wissenschaften*, XVI, I (1883), 179 ff. For his historical works see also B. A. Vermaseren *De katholieke nederlandsche geschiedschriving in de xvie en xviie eeuw* (1941), especially pp. 91–107.

[2] Aitzing inserted the cycle in or before 1581 in a very appropriate context where he had not used it in 1579 (see p. 139, n. 2, below). We know that some manuscript of Luigi da Porto was accessible about that time because two of the letters (Nos. 55 and 56) are printed in the first volume of *Lettere di principi*, in both editions (Venice, 1573–7 and 1581) of the three-volume collection, of which the second and third volumes were edited by Francesco and Girdano Ziletti. It is curious that Ranke did not recognize them when they reappeared in the edition of the *Lettere storiche*. Although in his *Geschichte der romanischen und germanischen Völker von 1494 bis 1514*, 3rd ed. (1885), p. 241, n. 4, he makes a good critical remark on the general character of the letters, he does not in the notes to pp. 251, 259 and 269 correct the error of the *Lettere di principi* which gives the writer's Christian name as Leonardo.

of propagandist historians, who worked for the restoration of Spanish authority by writing accounts of the events in the Netherlands from the loyalist point of view. Aitzing gave them assistance; but in his own historical work he was markedly unlike them.

He was and avowed himself a Catholic, but, unlike his polemizing friends, he aimed at impartiality and sometimes he censured the acts of his own side. His topographical and historical folio on the Netherlands revolt, *De leone belgico*,[1] is in the main a dry and colourless collection of facts, which still derives a certain value from the care with which he states exactly when and where each event occurred. One of his old Antwerp associates enriched the book with engravings. Most of these are pictures, more or less imaginary, of historical scenes; but there are two which are symbolical. One of these, the title-page, provides a key to the whole work.[2]

Very few modern readers have the patience to interpret the symbols in it, but it does immediately show a reason for Aitzing's attentiveness to times and places and also for his impartiality. He was an astrologer. The celestial influences which Luigi da Porto mentioned in casual asides seemed to him to be matters for painstaking research. He believed that history was full of exact chronological repetitions, with similar events occurring at exactly equal intervals of time.

---

[1] The earliest edition was published in 1581; the earliest which I have seen carries the story down to 1583 and was published in Cologne, presumably in 1584: except that a continuation is added, the edition which includes the events of 1585 is identical.

[2] The other is a map in which the details of the Netherlands are accurately plotted, but the outline is represented in the shape of a lion, a conceit which was afterwards adopted in the title-pages of the most popular of all the Catholic histories of the Netherlands revolt, the *De bello belgico* (1632–47) of the Jesuit Strada.

Even we ourselves have our little superstitions and observances about birthdays, anniversaries, jubilees, centenaries, lucky days, coincidences of dates and the like. These are survivals of what once were serious scientific beliefs. In the sixteenth century, when impressive new mathematical discoveries were being made, and the knowledge of mathematics was spreading to wider circles, no one was sure how far the significance of times and numbers might extend. There was at least one author who compiled a short history of the world in the form of a calendar of anniversaries for every day in the year.[1] Aitzing represented this way of thinking in a much more complicated form. He combined in an elaborate system all these things, together with others from astrology, with chronograms and interpretations of the names and initials of patriarchs and emperors.

As a young man he had written a curious little book called *Pentaplus Regnorum Mundi*,[2] a title which may almost be translated as 'the fivefold course of history'. It is a guide, on these cabalistic principles, to all history, past, present and future, with folding tables and elaborate indexes. It shows the cyclical movement (*progressio circularis*) of all kings, kingdoms and times, and the author firmly writes: 'Quid est quod fuit? ipsum quod futurum est. Quid est quod factum est? ipsum quod est faciendum.'[3] The Emperor Ferdinand I commended Aitzing to Pope Pius IV, and said in his letter that this book not only corrected the chronology of former historians, but furthermore attempted to link the movements of the heavenly bodies above with the vicissi-

[1] Ludovico Dolce, *Giornale delle historie del mondo* (Venice, 1572).
[2] Stieve dated the first edition, which he had not seen, 1561 or 1562. I have seen only the enlarged Plantin edition of 1579.
[3] P. 14, quoting Eccles. i. 9.

tudes of kingdoms and empires below, by an admirable and very simple system (*mira quadam ratione, eaque facillima*), and yet in such a way that these vicissitudes were referred in the last resort to the unchanging will of God.[1]

In the light of our scientific knowledge, subsequently acquired, we can be certain that this apparatus is worthless, and that it was worthless when it was constructed, except that it provided Aitzing with a motive, though the wrong motive, for his conscientious precision. It is, however, rather surprising that the book did not make his fortune. According to the standards of the time it deserved respectful attention, and, more than that, in itself it was genuinely scientific. It resulted from an attempt to understand the nature of succession in time, and when he came to write on the Netherlands, Aitzing used it to set his contemporary history in the framework of universal history. The prefatory matter in this book on the Netherlands includes a table of dates from Adam to the days of Philip II of Spain, with which the body of the work begins. The symbolic title-page is an improved version of the title-page of the *Pentaplus*.[2] It is followed by twenty-four pages of explanation, and, at the end of the book, besides two tabular calendars, there are indexes which enable the reader to find the lunar date of any event, and the events in Old Testament and New Testament history which correspond to it in this scheme.

It is on the title-page that Aitzing first presents the cycle of war and peace. The design shows, to the right and left, two Tuscan pillars, with letters running down them, and

[1] This letter is prefixed to the book.

[2] In the dedication of the second part of the *Pentaplus* to the Emperor Rudolph II (p. 43 in the edition of 1579) it is announced that a full explanation of the title-page will be given in the forthcoming book on the Belgian lion.

with columns of figures beside them. Above them are the sun and the moon, joined by a rainbow, also mysteriously scored with figures. In the four corners are the lion, the bear, the leopard and the eagle which represent the four historic monarchies, Assyrian, Persian, Greek and Roman. Between the pillars there is a circle, inscribed within a square, and round this circle or 'rotating wheel' (*rota conversionis*) as the author calls it, six words are engraved: Pax, Ubertas, Luxus, Bellum, Pauperies, Luctus. Each faces its opposite diagonally; peace is at the top and war at the bottom.[1] Three times in the course of the book the idea is applied to the events in the Netherlands. The six words describe the six *ditiones*, regimes we might say, which succeeded one another there in the period from 1559. Under Margaret of Parma plenty passed over into luxury and war; under the Duke of Alva there was poverty; under Requesens lamentation; Don John of Austria made peace, or rather (for the adjustment seems sadly defective) there would have been peace in the time of his successor, Alexander Farnese, if it had not been for the suspicions of his enemies. In fact the situation at the time of going to press was parallel to that described in the eleventh chapter of the Book of Zechariah, when the lion was roaring and the king had two rods in his hand, one for peace and the other for war.[2]

About the end of the seventeenth century the notion of the cycle of war and peace appears once more, and this time in a form which definitely seems to imply some relation to the

[1] The diagram given by Vermaseren, p. 105, is his own: the spokes of the wheel are inserted, and the positions are moved round.

[2] Fol. 25 b. See also the Epilogue, p. 508. In the edition of 1588 (continued to 1587) the preliminary summary is on p. 5 and is rearranged so that not the rulers but the phases are numbered. The Epilogue is dropped.

words of Luigi da Porto. Surprisingly enough it appears in America. It appears as a motto on one of the title-pages of 'The Beehive', an enormous manuscript commonplace-book in seven languages kept by Francis Daniel Pastorius. Pastorius was a German, bred to the law, who studied in four universities and was one of the Frankfurt circle of Philipp Jakob Spener, the founder of pietism. He came into contact with the Quakers, and settled in America, where he founded Germantown in Pennsylvania and was a noteworthy figure among the Friends. He seems to have had a sense of remoteness from Europe and its learning, and to have copied useful passages from his reading mainly for the instruction of his family, adding a few reflexions of his own. Among them is this quatrain:

> War begets Poverty, Poverty Peace
> Then people will traffic and Riches increase
> Riches produceth Pride, Pride is War's ground,
> War begets Poverty, So we go round.[1]

Here pride is mentioned, as it was by da Porto, though, perhaps through the exigencies of metre, there is nothing about anger or humanity. Nor is there anything about the stars. By the time of Pastorius, Galileo and Newton had written; Halley had calculated the orbit of his comet;

---

[1] This is quoted by E. A. J. Johnson, *American Economic Thought in the Eighteenth Century*, p. 100, from the periodical *America Germanica* (1897), 1. I have not been able to find a copy of this periodical in England. The best authority on Pastorius is M. D. Learned's *Life of Francis Daniel Pastorius* (1908), where the 'Beehive', which was begun in 1696, is described on pp. 241–54: there is nothing in the lists of sources there given which shows whence he got the idea of the cycle. It was Mr Learned who published the extracts in *America Germanica*, and I suppose that it was from here that it found its way into another book where it appears without acknowledgement, a collection of extracts for recitation, of which, perhaps fortunately, I have forgotten the title.

astrology had lost its scientific status, and reputable thinkers no longer tried to connect terrestrial history with the motions of the heavens.

This is not the end of the literary history of this special form of the idea, but we need not follow it further. We have seen it sink from the level of science to that of proverbial philosophy; but in forms appropriate to the intellectual habits of our own time it is still current in serious historical works. Just as Aitzing fitted the cycle of war and peace into his more general cyclical doctrine, there are modern writers who fit it into their theories of cycles. Ten years ago, for instance, a British economist published a thoughtful article on 'War and the Trade Cycle'. It was illustrated with a graph showing the exact dates of certain wars and the percentages of unemployment during and between them. There was also a summary table of the movements of prices. The last paragraph began:

> The conclusion is that the wars of the last century have tended to break out about the peaks of cyclical activity, but only in those cycles which occurred in the more prosperous long periods. Is prosperity the mother of wars? The most we can say on these facts alone is that there is a dangerous economic conjuncture centring round the peaks of economic activity.[1]

Without statistical investigation we ought not to carry this train of thought further; but if we were to do so we might perhaps be led to conclude that war brings about another conjuncture, centring round the troughs of economic activity, which is favourable to peace. We should then have

---

[1] *Glasgow Herald*, 31 March 1938. This article is anonymous, but the argument closely resembles that of a longer article by A. L. Macfie in *Economic History*, III (1938), 89 ff. Its purpose is to refute the even less plausible view that the dangerous conjuncture is at times of depression.

confirmed the opinion of Luigi da Porto except for what he wrote about pride, anger and humanity, factors which cannot be handled statistically in the present state of knowledge. For progress in that direction we must await further development of encephalography, the new electrical technique which records the movements of emotion in the brain.

In spite of their differences of language and content and context the four passages which I have quoted are alike not only in some of the words they use but also in stating that there is a cycle of war and peace, and that it works through economic prosperity and impoverishment. None of them tells us whether these must affect both sides in a war or whether it is enough for one of them to become rich or poor. They draw no distinctions whatever between the two parties to a quarrel. They are impartial in the sense that it is irrelevant to their truth or falsity whether one belligerent is an aggressor, whether the war is just or unjust. The economist, the most abstract of the four, entirely omits the psychological or moral links which the others include in the chain of causation: his conclusion might be equally true of 'the bickerings of kites and crows'. In each instance we can easily see why this is so. War came into the life of Luigi da Porto and Michael von Aitzing as an interruption from outside, and they were accustomed to thinking that men were at the mercy of distant and indifferent powers. Pastorius looked on with the detachment of the exile and the pacifist. The economist sought for quantitative expressions of the course of events. Any cyclical view of history implies that a situation recurs which is identical in all the points that are relevant to the matter it explains. The fewer the points which are regarded as relevant, the easier, therefore, it will be to detect historical cycles, and an abstract view of history, which disregards all but a few selected phenomena, will easily fall into such a scheme. Each of our four writers gives an abstract statement, which will have just as much, or as little, truth in it whatever are the concrete circumstances of the beginning and the end of each actual war.

The way in which the cycle of war and peace appears in their writings is an example of something that we often meet with in the history of thought. First, there is an idea which gets rough-and-ready expression and passes current in speech; someone writes it down and connects it loosely with the accepted opinions of the day; a second writer straightens it out and uses it as an element in a systematic interpretation of some body of data; but afterwards, when the theoretical framework of his interpretation has become obsolete, nothing remains of the idea except the original unscientific core. After an interval another author, interested in the data for entirely different reasons, picks up this core and examines its shape to see whether it will fit into his own hypotheses.[1] Thus an interpretative idea about the course of history may be essentially the same although it appears in different systems of thought. When this is so we may form our judgement on the validity of the idea without paying attention to its origin and development. We are entitled to ignore the masses of information which too often smother the critical elements in the history of ideas.

The idea of the cycles of war and peace is a case in point: we may examine it as it is in itself, apart from any system

[1] As a parallel example we might take the theory of the trade-cycle, from the time when Montesquieu wrote: 'Il arrive tous les dix ans des révolutions qui précipitent le riche dans le misère et enlèvent le pauvre, avec des ailes rapides, au comble des richesses' (*Lettres persanes*, 1721, XLVIII).

into which it may, as people say nowadays, be integrated. We may ask whether it fits the facts as historians know them. We can easily find instances which are not in accordance with it. Poverty does not always and automatically bring peace: no one can believe that who has understood the last ten years in Europe. Nor must belligerents always be impoverished before they come to terms: no such thing happened in the six weeks' war of 1866 between Prussia and Austria. The cycle is over-simplified. When we have proved this, however, we have not disposed of it. Inaccuracies do not invalidate an argument, and we ought to go further and ask whether there is any truth left in it when we have made every allowance for errors and exceptions. Let us then try to compare the cyclical theory with the ascertained results of historical study.

One such result, far more familiar now than it was in England a generation ago, is that the distinction between war and peace is not absolute. The relations of states or civil factions, or other bodies which may come into conflict, are not such that there must be either war or peace between them and there cannot be a mixture of the two. This obvious truth has been brought home to us in recent years by an extensive experience of undeclared wars and of disturbances in times of nominal peace; but it was stated three hundred years ago: 'As the nature of foule weather, lyeth not in a showre or two of rain; but in an inclination thereto of many days together: so the nature of war, consisteth not in actuall fighting; but in the known disposition thereto, during all the time there is no assurance to the contrary.'[1] We might, indeed, concede all this and yet maintain some

[1] Thomas Hobbes, *Leviathan* (1651), p. 62.

cyclical theory, but we could not believe in a process in which the nominal, legal or apparent beginning or ending of a state of war had any cardinal significance. The dates to which Aitzing and the economist paid so much attention are irrelevant to the question how and why wars come about. I believe it could be shown that many of the apparently philosophical or scientific wrappings in which theories of history are presented to us nowadays are equally irrelevant. What we can easily see to be true of the mathematical fancies of the sixteenth century may well be applied to the biological analogies or the psychological dogmas of the present day.

There is another principle which, though not altogether incompatible with a cyclical process, is very hard to reconcile with anything so abstract, the principle that the causes of war change with the changes in the life of society. However much we may disagree about the nature of social causation in general, or about the specific causes of this war or that war, we ought to accept this as proved. The conscious aims of political leaders, their unconscious motives, and the inducements by which they have brought organized masses of men into battle, have always been relative to social conditions. Historians have disputed much about these matters. Herodotus, the oldest of the historians whose works we still possess, began his book by announcing in the first sentence that he would record the great things that happened among the Greeks and the barbarians, and especially through what cause, δι' ἣν αἰτίην, they made war on one another. He was not satisfied with the accepted explanation, and he improved upon it. So it has been ever since. In our own time historians discuss whether there ever were any wars for religion, and whether there were wars of liberation which had no economic motives. In all these controversies both sides assume that the test of an explanation is whether it agrees with what we know about the societies in which the wars were made.

This analysis of the causes of war is one of the links which connect historical with sociological studies. Much of it is to be found in theoretical and generalized books which have little to say about individual statesmen or other human beings, and these books are part of a wider literature, often of a deterministic tinge, in which, even when there are human figures in the foreground, it is assumed that the great movements of society are out of their control. The popularity of Tolstoy's great masterpiece in Britain and America during the recent war seemed to prove that many educated people have no aversion, at least in a work of genius describing an admired ally, from a theory of war and peace which removes them altogether from the sphere of human choice.

Is it not a very striking fact that the historians who have contributed most to our knowledge of these matters, such as the historians of diplomacy, have based their work on quite opposite assumptions? Instead of following economic trends they have minutely dissected treaties and dispatches. They scrutinize the mind of each of their characters at each moment, asking what did he know, what did he believe, what did he expect, what did he want, what did he say and to whom did he say it, what did he do? They try to establish precisely what part each individual played in each transaction. By so doing they have brought together an immense co-ordinated body of conclusions. These are, as we have admitted that all historical conclusions must be, hypothetical. Every scientific thinker must be prepared for occasions when his data can no longer be explained by the hypotheses on which he is working, and when, in order to cover new accessions of knowledge, he must formulate new hypotheses; but if we look at this body of knowledge as a whole and in detail, I believe we ought to judge that its assumptions are still valid. It is on these hypotheses that we must continue to build our studies of war and peace.

To work thus, in terms of individual minds and wills, of freedom and responsibility, is to adhere to the main tradition of Western thought. Those ideas which have their most finished expression in the theological and legal doctrines of what constitutes a just war, all assume that wars come about in consequence of the choice of free and responsible agents. It is, indeed, very rarely that the individuals who decide are few in number. Nearly always, even in societies much simpler than our own, they are very many. Nor do they often decide by a rational choice, a balancing of considerations on one side and the other in the light of reason alone. In this matter, above all others, we know how great a part is played by the irrational elements in human nature. The formula of Clausewitz, that war is a continuation of policy by other means, is shallow and rationalistic if it means that at a given moment, without any change in their purposes, men decide to resort to the use of force. But it is neither shallow nor rationalistic to say that every one of the innumerable decisions which ultimately lead to war is a moral choice, a choice in which reason ought to be heeded, a choice in which justice and mercy, right and wrong are relevant to the issue. By no ingenuity can the historical process, as this tradition understands it, or as the diplomatic historians record it, be interpreted as a cyclical process. The circle, with its imperceptible movements from one direction to another, is the least appropriate figure for this world of conflict and manœuvre which the experts explain to us in terms of personality and purpose.

Creighton, in his historical works, belonged to this tradition. He took history as he found it. He was not misled, like some of his most eminent contemporaries, by the illusion of general progress. He wrote in a letter: 'We will never get rid of war.'[1] But, if he accepted war as an accompaniment of life in society, it was not in a spirit of indifference or detachment. He was gifted with sympathetic imagination which enabled him to enter into the experiences of his historical characters. 'I try to put myself in their place: to see their limitations, and leave the course of events to pronounce the verdict on system and men alike.'[2] He believed that this verdict was followed by a judgement. To accept war in this way as an incident of human nature is not the same thing as saying that it comes by a uniform, necessary process. Indeed, the two things cannot both be true. May we not conclude that wars do not come and go according to a rhythm of their own of which wise men ought merely to be stoical spectators, and may we not claim Creighton as an ally in so concluding?

[1] *Life and Letters*, II, 403.
[2] *Ibid.* II, 376.

POSTSCRIPT

On p. 134, above, I wrote that Luigi da Porto did not claim to have invented his version of the cycle. After this lecture was published, Dr Henry F. Schwarz very kindly wrote to me from Wellesley College, Massachusetts, and drew my attention to an earlier and very interesting example of it. This is on p. 576 of the first volume of Joseph Chmel, *Geschichte Kaiser Friedrichs des IV und seines Sohns Maximilian* (1840), and comes on the first folio of the diary written by Frederick IV with his own hand, and printed there. From its position it seems likely to be roughly contemporary with an entry opposite to it, which notes his beginning to reign in 1435 at the age of twenty. Along with it are proverbs, Biblical and other quotations, lists of names, jottings of cash spent in Venice, recipes, the Greek alphabet, the Arabic numerals, and suchlike miscellanea, notably current sayings about love and fortune in Latin and German. All this makes it seem very unlikely that Frederick devised the jingle himself. His version of it runs: 'frid macht reichtum reichtum macht hochfart hochfart macht unainigung unainigung macht diemutikait diemutikait macht frid.' It may be possible to trace earlier sources for it in Austria or in North Italy. In any case it belongs to a large family of similar cycles, dealing with various matters but perhaps all akin to the idea of the wheel of fortune, which goes back to classical antiquity.

LIST OF BOOKS AND ARTICLES

In the footnotes to the foregoing lectures works by the author are referred to by their numbers in this list. It gives the titles of all books and articles by the author which bear on the subject of the lectures, except reviews, articles subsequently incorporated in the books and articles which he does not now consider to have any further value for this subject. In several of those mentioned in the list, subjects touched on in the lectures are treated more at length and with fuller references to authorities.

1. *The Dutch Alliance and the War against French Trade, 1688–97* (1923).

2. 'War trade and trade war, 1701–1713', in *Economic History Review*, I (1927).

3. 'Neutral commerce in the War of the Spanish Succession and the Treaty of Utrecht', in *British Year Book of International Law* (1928).

4. 'Edward Grimeston, the translator', in *English Historical Review*, XLIII (1928).

5. 'Anglo-Dutch relations of commercial policy and the Nine Years War of 1688–1697', in *Verslag van de Algemeene Vergadering der Leden van het Historisch Genootschap gehowden te Utrecht* (1932).

6. *The Seventeenth Century* (1929), second edition 1947, especially chapters VI–X which deal with armies, navies, international law and diplomacy, and the interests of the states.

7. *The Later Stuarts* (1934), second edition 1955.

8. *Guide to English Commercial Statistics, 1696–1782* (Royal Historical Society, Guides and Handbooks, no. 1, 1938).

Appendix

9. Introductions to *Minutes of the Hudson's Bay Company, 1679–1684* (Champlain Society and Hudson's Bay Record Society), First Part 1945, Second Part, 1946.

10. *The Colonial Conferences between England and the Netherlands in 1613 and 1615*, part II (Bibliotheca Visseriana, vol. XVII, 1951). The two parts of this work both appear under the names of G. N. Clark and Jonkheer W. J. M. van Eysinga. They were written in consultation but separately by the two writers.

11. 'The character of the Nine Years War', in *Cambridge Historical Journal*, XI (1954). This was written after the revision of pp. 167–8 of no. 7 above for the second edition, and mentions an alternative to the traditional view there expressed.

INDEX

Index

Index

Index

Index